EVERYTHING I KNOW ABOUT WOMEN, I LEARNED FROM MY TRACTOR

ROGER WELSCH

MBI

This edition published in 2003. First published in 2002 by MBI Publishing Company, Galtier Plaza, Suite 200, 380 Jackson Street, St. Paul, MN 55101-3885 USA

Motorbooks International titles are also available at discounts in bulk quantity for industrial or sales-promotional use. For details write to Special Sales Manager at Motorbooks International Wholesalers & Distributors, Galtier Plaza, Suite 200, 380 Jackson Street, St. Paul, MN 55101-3885 USA.

ISBN 0-7603-1627-9

Printed in the United States of America

Contents

A COMPLETE MAN'S ENCYCLOPAEDIC GUIDE IN 47 VOLUMES

By Roger Welsch

Man School Professor Emeritus and Extraordinaire, Bon Vivant, Raconteur, Connoisseur, Master Mechanic, Generalist in Affairs de Coeur, Expert in Matters Feminine, Love Doctor, Noted Romantic, Explicator of Female Arcana, Decipherer of the Woman School Codes of Conduct

Being a Man School textbook complete with real-life examples, histories, cases, dialogues, anecdotes, parables, lessons, citations from and references to important and recognized authorities like W.C. Fields on picking up babes to engineering easy separations in personal relationships, designed to aid the human male in all manner of mixed-gender encounters and to deal with them successfully, which is to say, come out alive, at least in most cases.

Volume I of XLVII

When chapmen billes leave the street,
And drouthy neebors, neebors meet,
As market days are wearing late,
An' folk begin to tak the gate;
While we sit bousing at the nappy,
And getting fou and unco happy,
We think na on the lang Scots miles,
The mosses, waters, slaps, and styles,
That lie between us and our hame,
Where sits our sulky sullen dame.
Gathering her brows like gathering storm,
Nursing her wrath to keep it warm.

—Robert Burns, about Roger Welsch, and you, and every other male who's ever had anything to do with a woman and spent an evening up at the town tavern with his buddies.

DEDICATION

For Dan, Bondo, Melvin, Mick, Eric, Dan, Izzy, John, Paul, Bill, Leon, Vic, Allen, Dick, Verne, Jay, Lucky, Thud, etc., all too male for their own good.

ACKNOWLEDGMENTS

I owe thanks to a lot of people in my life, and a lot of women, but discretion being the better part of valor, and Linda still thinking I came to her an innocent, I'm going to leave almost all those names out. I think I expressed my gratitude quite effusively at the time. But I can say many thanks to Paula Barbour at *Successful Farming*, Master Editor and Graduate Faculty Dean of Woman School, Iowa Division. And to Laurie, Cheryl, and Nancy, also of *Successful Farming* and also accomplished graduates of Woman School. And to Pam and Terry, Sue, Kay, Mary Ethel, LeAnn, Linda R., Lucy, and Dee, all of whom Linda knows about and with whom she shares Woman School updates and bulletins.

Especially to Antonia and Joyce, wonderful daughters who have been generous with information about Woman School, for example, The Sigh, covered in detail later.

Most of all, thanks to Lovely Linda, who does all the things a wife is expected to do within our culture and society, and all the things she is expected to do by her insensitive clod of a husband, and yet still remains one of the five or six wittiest people I have met in my 65 years of life. I'd be in real trouble if I didn't have Linda to steal from. Thank you, Linda, for your insights into Woman School and for applying that venerable institution's lessons gently enough not to kill me over the past two decades.

And thank you, Lovely Linda, for never having asked me to teach you how to load a pistol. That alone has brought me great peace of mind over the years.

The careful reader may have noticed that on the title page of this book, the volume is indicated to be Volume I. The book you hold in your hands is projected to be the first in a 47-volume series in which I will explain almost everything in the world. My old buddy, Mick Maun, may have carried things a bit too far in suggesting that my previous adventures into the theories of Woman School, especially *Love, Sex, and Tractors*, are, for all the world, in the same league as the Bible and should have been published as the Old Testament and New Testament of Man School.

But he was more on target with his follow-up recommendation that this series be published as an encyclopedia with annual updates on new information and discoveries. I think this plan will depend to some degree on the response from the Defense and Security Department of Woman School. If things turn violent, it's hard to say how much backbone any of us are willing to admit to.

But the theory is, Volume II is projected to provide guidance for men in the selection of automobiles and dogs, manners and protocol, travel advice and sartorial guidelines, health and hygiene, hunting and fishing techniques, selection of the best canoe for your purposes, lawn care rules, bonsai tree pruning, formulas for rotating radial tires, a complete listing of the firing order on various tractor engines, blueprints for building your own outhouse, how to eat artichokes, design plans for briefcase nuclear devices, recipes for perfect coffee, ferret training tricks, an outline of world history, the Big Bang theory, tactics of guerilla warfare, how to mix the perfect martini, a brief biography of Jim Harrison, 101 stink bait recipes, routes to and from Byzantium by way of the Silk Road, and how to make chokecherry jelly.

Volumes III–XLVII will explain how women think.

CHAPTER 1

WOMAN SCHOOL, MAN SCHOOL

Woman was God's second mistake.

—NIETZSCHE, *THE ANTICHRIST*

This is not a book of hypothetical theories. It is also not a mere compendium of random personal experiences. Nosirree. Every single male I know has gone through something roughly like the situations I am about to deal with in the following pages. Insofar as possible I have tried to provide precise and true examples from real life, as uncomfortable as they might make you feel. If you are new to dilemmas of dealing with women, study this textbook carefully. If you've been around the block a few times—well, get ready to nod your head vigorously about 6,000 times.

In several previous books, notably *Diggin' In & Piggin' Out* and *Love, Sex, and Tractors*, I casually mentioned the previously secret society of Woman School. In a way, that was only a test. I was sure Woman School existed, that place all women go to learn how to be a woman. Women are not born alike, yet ten years or so later, they all are alike. So, where do they learn all of these techniques, tricks, guises, ploys, gambits, and guile we men learn to know and fear?

Woman School, that's where!

Just as there is the thin blue line within law enforcement circles, a mutually protective but silent agreement of loyalty no matter what, there is also a pink line. No woman would admit to any male that there even is such a thing as Woman School, much less hint at where it is, how it works, what subjects are taught. My thought was that perhaps if I proceeded in the two books mentioned above (ostensibly about cooking and eating and working on antique tractors), simply assuming that Woman School is there, I might penetrate more deeply into its dark and arcane secrets.

This strategy worked. The fog cleared; women stumbled into my cleverly laid trap; the veil fell away; and while I still don't know everything about Woman School, I believe I know more than any other living male. This book is not so much an exploration of Woman School as it is an effort to provide my own species (men) with the tools and weapons to function on the same level of preparedness and organization as women. Gentlemen, this is your official textbook for Man School.

There are dangers. If this book should fall into a woman's hands, clearly any advantage of surprise will be lost to us. But I have seen men willing to change their names, crawl in the mud, surrender up a good dog in return for the privilege of kissing a woman's little pinkie fingernail, so I have no illusions about how fast this text is going to wind up in feminine hands. No matter. Once we all have this information, we have it.

Even in *Diggin' In* and *Love, Sex, and Tractors*, I knew I was revealing enough about men that there was some risk of weakening our position. But our strength, my pals and buddies, is not in secrecy. Moreover, I simply don't know how to get the enclosed information out to you while maintaining top security.

I hoped to make my previous books available only to male purchasers, but this thing about the Constitution came up, and the flap with the National Organization of Women, and then Oprah, and Doctor Laura. Man, that got really ugly. I once mentioned to Lovely Linda, my wife (and I suspect a dean in Woman School) that perhaps I would make *Love, Sex, and Tractors* available for sale to women only if they had written permission from an adult male. "And just where are we supposed to find one of those?" she asked snippily.

So, ladies, here it is. Read it if you want. I know you'll read it no matter what we want. But don't try to deny there is Woman School. Your cover has been blown. Some of your sisters were outwitted by my own clever wiles, and the cat is out of the bag.

THE OATH

Perhaps the most stunning insight I have gotten about Woman School came to me quite unexpectedly. I was conversing with a very intelligent, highly placed woman about something totally apart from anything to do with Woman School, when she suddenly looked up and met my eyes. She paused a moment and said, "Rog, I am willing to tell you the first five words of the Woman School Oath."

I was flabbergasted. To this day I don't know what motivated her to betray her sisters and her own vow of secrecy. As I recall, I didn't even respond. I didn't know what to say. As it turns out, I didn't have to say a word. Perhaps sensing my total astonishment, she continued, "The first five words of the Woman School Oath are: 'Let the man believe that . . ..'"

Even as that utterly unexpected information soaked in, she went on, "And then there's a long list of various things—a long list."

That woman has never said more to me about Woman School, or about that moment when she opened her soul and showed pity for not only this one poor wretch of a man but for all mankind. The conclusions we can draw from this are: 1) there is a Woman School Oath, therefore, 2) there is a Woman School, and 3) I guess they're letting us believe something or other.

WOMAN SCHOOL CURRICULUM

Other women have stumbled and made explicit reference to Woman School, perhaps thinking I could be trusted, perhaps thinking it was too late because I already knew about Woman School, perhaps thinking that as a kindly, unassuming old gentleman, I was no threat. Perhaps because the woman in question loved me.

For example, just days ago one of the most beloved women in my life, daughter Antonia, slipped and made specific, explicit, clear reference not only to the existence of Woman School but to the nature of its curriculum. Without further comment, I am going to duplicate here her exact message to me. Read it. Let it soak in. Does it sound at all familiar? Does this explain certain events with women in your own life? Is this an answer to a couple thousand of your own questions?

I had tried to help Antonia in a tight situation, a personal fix. I thought the advice of an older, loving friend might be of use to her. It wasn't. This is what she wrote:

> *Dad!*
>
> *Here is a quick lesson to help you out:*
>
> *By not getting involved you got involved. (This situation slightly resembles the yes/no principle . . . yes means no, no means no in all cases where no does not mean yes, and maybe means yes, but sometimes also no.) When you didn't answer the phone, you got involved. If you had answered the phone you would have, indeed, gotten involved. There is a certain beauty about the situation, isn't there?*
>
> *Take everything with a grain of salt, for we are women and do occasionally tend to roar at whoever or whatever is there at the time.*
>
> *I would like to hope that we can all forget about this and act like it didn't happen (sort of like the '80s, certain bean dishes, and Spandex) so don't answer this letter with a statement of what happened, or an explanation. I have moved forward and care not to look back right now. I hope you aren't*

7

stewing, even though I know you are, and I will continue not to stew even though, undoubtedly, you know I am.

I love you, Daddy, and I hope all is well.

Love, your sugar plum,
Antonia

P.S. REMEMBER: yes means no, no means no in all cases where no does not mean yes, and maybe means yes, but sometimes also no.

Take it from me, therefore, there is a Woman School. They have an oath but their code of silence can be broken. And a slick, sneaky, sly, fearless, experienced son of a gun like me is precisely the kind of guy who's going to do it. In these pages you will share the first few mortar rounds of this new war. (Or maybe rear-guard action would be a more appropriate turn of phrase.)

PATTERNS

It's not as if no one has previously noticed the patterns produced by Woman School. We see the results of that training program around us all the time but very few men have put the pieces together and figured out that there is indeed a formal and requisite program, rigorously taught and attended by all women. This confusion is facilitated by the agreement that women never talk about their training at this school. Men stumble through life thinking all these identical behaviors are a matter of coincidence.

For example, a friend and colleague of mine from my years with CBS, Andy Rooney, has written about a phenomenon that is clearly a product of Woman School. But despite his rich experience, fine education, and very sharp mind, he speaks of it as if it were something that simply dropped from the sky into the minds of women everywhere. "My wife uses fabric softener. I never knew what that stuff was for. Then I noticed women coming up to me [sniff] "Married" [walk off]. That's how they mark their territory. You can take off the ring, but it's hard to get that April-fresh scent out of your clothes."

There is no doubt. This is a lesson of Woman School.

Another subtle clue about the existence of Woman School came to me once when I was lamenting to Lovely Linda that an old friend of mine was about to get married. Like another friend recently married, this gent was elderly, his wife had passed away, and many of us thought he was remarrying much too quickly, driven more by his loneliness than good sense.

"I just hope he doesn't wind up like Marvin [not his real name, I hasten to note], with this new woman in his life cutting him off from his friends, from the tavern, from driving around the country-side, from living the life he has always lived so happily. I just hope this marriage doesn't make him miserable like ol' Marv."

Without looking up from her embroidery, Linda said, "Why should he be any different from the rest of you?"

"The rest of you . . . " How does Linda know about the rest of us? Because she is part of a huge conspiracy, and the foundation of that organized perfidy is Woman School!

THE EVIDENCE ACCUMULATES

If you look around you, you will begin to see dozens, hundreds, maybe thousands of clear indications not only that there is a Woman School but, what kinds of lessons are taught at that institution. The evidence for Woman School is everywhere, manifest and manifold. Watch the women in your life. Whenever a woman, or several women, do something or say something that leaves you just a touch baffled, ask yourself where she, or they, could have learned this behavior. Not from you. Not in school. Not from television. Not in church. Nope, she learned it in Woman School.

Again, let me turn to my own experience, and my own woman child. A man perhaps has no better way of learning inadvertently the deepest secrets of Woman School than through a woman child. Not long ago my family was driving into a city of some size and along the way we went through a very ritzy district of very large, very handsome homes. Daughter Antonia, then fifteen years old, pointed to one of the mansions and said calmly, "When I grow up, Dad, I'm going to live in a house like that."

Fine with Dad. I thought, however, I would try to extract a lesson from this grand dream. "What do you intend to do in your life so you wind up in a place like that?" I asked, expecting—thinking like a man—that she would perhaps consider sound investment, hard work, clean living. But no. She had already been to Woman School, unbeknownst to her father. Without a second's thought, she said, "Divorce a doctor."

Not *marry* a doctor. No, *divorce* a doctor. That is clearly a lesson straight out of Woman School.

Another example of a technique Antonia clearly acquired at Woman School.

ANTONIA: [*Leaving the house for school*] "Dad, I'm going to stop on the way home and have my hair cut."

DAD: [*Mystified*] "Uh . . . okay."

ANTONIA: "Dad, I'm telling you that so when I come home you can pretend to notice."

THE CONSPIRACY

I am surrounded, *besieged*, by women. My mother was a woman. I have at least three daughters, and a granddaughter, and I have had two wives. My editor at *Successful Farming* is a woman; the editor at Motorbooks who will assemble an index for this book is a woman. Women. Everywhere. Which is to say, I've had enough experience here to know what I am talking about. It is not that I have any special powers or unusual insights. You too can detect the lessons of Woman School if you only consider where the women in your life could have learned what they know. And when and where there is a clear collusion between women, it almost always contributes to the control, if not subjugation of men.

Woman School alumnae ties are very strong. It's not as if women graduate and then go out into the world and about their business independently. The bonds are strong and the loyalties deep. That's the secret: women are intensely educated at Woman School, but then the coordination within the female system remains very strong and active for the rest of their lives.

Once again, I am not the sort of researcher who unloads a wagonload of guesswork and moves on. Nope, I have plenty of evidence. For example, not long ago I was looking for something in our clothes closet when I discovered a shoebox with three lace doilies and $3,008 in cash in it. Curious, I took the box downstairs, showed it to Linda, and asked if she knew anything about it. A bit abashed she said yes, it was her box.

She then revealed just a bit of how Woman School operates. She said that on our wedding day, her mother had taken her aside and told her that any time she got thoroughly fed up with me, sick and tired of my maleness, and was pushed to the brink of murder or abandonment, she should do what she herself had done in her own marriage: tat a doily. She said the focus on making a doily removed the frustration and anger she was feeling. It was this activity that had saved her own marriage with Jake many, many times.

Linda confessed that she had, therefore, followed the same course, making a doily when she was completely sick and tired of me. Three doilies in twenty years. Not bad, but what about the $3,008? Where did it come from?

"From selling doilies," she said.

CURRICULAR MATERIALS OF
WOMAN SCHOOL

The study in your hand constitutes only a preliminary, pioneering exploration of what exactly goes on at Woman School, what is taught and learned, the techniques, workshops, seminars, refresher courses, and field trips. Such Woman School tools are often hidden or disguised in such a way that they may be in plain sight, but not recognizable by the casual male observer.

For example, just this past week I noticed Linda was reading the book *Dog Training for Dummies*. Linda has no interest in training dogs. I peeked over her shoulder and could see that she was studying—even annotating and underlining—the section titled "Establishing Yourself As the Alpha Bitch." I asked her about it: "Why are you reading that, Linda?"

Her chilling response was, "No reason."

Yeah sure—a book about establishing yourself as the alpha bitch—that's just the kind of thing you're going to pick up and read for fun on a winter's evening.

SNUBB

In Woman School, female humans are taught a variety of techniques for dealing with men. Perhaps the most common, and yet most effective technique is what I have chosen to call the Rat Maze. I have some information, not altogether reliable however, that at Woman School and in the Woman School Man-ual [sic] it is identified as SNUBB: Situation Normal: Uninformed Bozo Baffled.

Here's the situation: You learn information that is certain to distress the woman in your life. Let's say you found out that your former girlfriend was in town earlier in the week, and she was asking about you. Your informant also told you that your ex was looking mighty fine and seemed to be curious about you in what could be interpreted as positive terms: "Does he still work on tractors? Is he still married to that witch? Does his distinguished gray hair still tumble coyly around his delicate ears like ocean waves over an abalone shell?" That kind of thing.

You know your current squeeze is not going to be at all happy that this representative of your irresponsible youth is not only alive, but within scratching distance. She certainly is not going to be amused that your former relationship hasn't withered away like a prune in the desert heat. And when she hears that this seductress who was never good enough for you in the first place even remembers that you have ears... well, this is not going to be a pretty situation. There are going to be ugly repercussions, no matter how innocent you happen to be, and hey, what are the chances of your being innocent, after all? She was a real hottie back then, and what could it hurt just to get together over a couple of drinks and recall old times, right?

Don't expect the current woman in your life to understand this logic. No, not at all.

There are ways to defuse an uncomfortable and potentially dangerous scenario like this, but it takes a good deal of foresight and planning on the part of the male. He would really have to be smart, worldly, woman-wise, suave, and experienced. Sort of like me. Before I walk you through how you might deal with this kind of emotional minefield, let me show you how I cleverly worked one.

A PRACTICAL EXAMPLE

A professional acquaintance recently admitted that she was in trouble with her husband because when he came home late one night and was crawling into bed beside her, she muttered my name, as in "Oh, Roger . . . Ooooooh Rog . . . .ooooh . . . . Ooooooh!" In a kind of orgasmic ecstasy, you know. (Now she protests that the words were groaned more in a spirit of anger and frustration, but I think we know what the truth is, right?) Anyway, I took this information to Linda immediately, figuring honesty is the best policy. And because we're being honest, I'll admit that I figured she'd find out sooner or later anyway so I better release the incriminating information under a controlled circumstance, like when I could see both her hands and had an excellent idea where all the household's handguns were.

Linda coolly listened to my story and with incredible control of her raging jealousy said, without so much as looking up from her embroidery, "Great. I could use the break. Tell her she can have you Tuesdays, Thursdays, and every other weekend."

I think she handled that well. Which means I handled it well. Which is to say, no one got hurt. Which is to say, I didn't get hurt.

PREEMPTIVE COUNTERSTRIKES

But, okay, back to this situation I have suggested to you: ex-girlfriend in town, you're wondering if you should say anything to the Little Lady, who looks a lot bigger when she's really pissed. What should you do in this situation?

1) Tell her the whole story up front because you know how angry she can be when you keep such information from her.
2) Don't tell her anything because you know how angry she can be when she hears information like this.
3) Attempt a diplomatic course with a set of subtle hints alluding to the information (see below):

   "I heard someone was in town asking about me."

   [*Pause to wait for response that might indicate she knows more than you hope.*]

   "Redhead . . . big boobs . . . fancy car."

   [*Pause. Pretend to read newspaper.*]

   "I see the Lutheran Church handi-bus has a new set of mud tires."

   [*Pause. Turn newspaper page.*]

   "You know, now that I think about it . . . I wonder if it wasn't Heather."

   [*Pause a really long time. Listen for increasingly deep breathing, mumbling . . . the click of ammo dropping into a snub-nose .38 Special.*]

"Of course, I doubt it was her. Last I heard, she was happily married to that Viking god she met at the spa."

If you don't have any response at this point, you are still apparently safe and yet you have laid a groundwork of honest candor in case this matter comes up again.

4) Enlist in the Marines.

Take your time in deciding which of these four courses of action is best for you. Consider the alternatives. Don't try to think of the most ethical approach, or the most expedient, or certainly the first one that appeals to you. As a male, you can pretty much be certain that kind of thinking is going to get you into nothing but trouble.

Incidentally, the right answer is none of the above.

SEMPER FUTILITY

In fact, none of any possibilities anywhere will work in any situation. The world-famous existentialist philosopher Red Green once said, "There are two theories about how to deal with women. Neither one works." Red Green is absolutely right: there is no right answer. Whatever course you choose in this matter, or any other matter, as long as there is a woman involved, you are going to be wrong, wrong, wrong, and you are going to suffer, suffer, suffer no matter what you say or do. Your goose is cooked, the die is cast, le jeux sont faites, ipse dixit, sotto voce, Deutschland ueber Alles. It's over.

LISTEN TO A GUY WHO'S BEEN THERE

If you tell this woman all the truth about your ex being in town and that you're considering having a good-ol'-days chat with her, she's going to be furious that you even know such information. If you don't tell, you are hiding things from her. If you try to be tactful, you are devious. If you enlist in the Marines, you are irresponsible. So, your only recourse is to crawl on your belly, plead masculinity, buy roses and chocolates. Do not threaten to slash your wrists because there is some chance she will think it over and help you out with the chore later that night as you lie whimpering and groaning in your guilt-ridden sleep.

The bottom line is that I struggled with my dilemma on my own. The puny intellectual efforts of one man, alone, without reference or guide. But Linda was moving within an enormous context, with information gathered in advanced Woman School seminars and with the total cooperation of the other woman in the story.

Guys, we don't have a chance, unless we: 1) come to grips with the reality of Woman School, and 2) begin to instruct our own kind in the ways and wiles of woman. We have been solitary, helpless prey standing resigned within a circle of predators. Until now. Until I wrote this book.

I can imagine you doubting my theory of an international female conspiracy. Well, believe me, I did not come to this horrible conclusion lightly. I wrote to several women with whom I work and mentioned something about being confused, and without exception, every single one of them, said something like, "Good. That's precisely what I had in mind. I guess it's working." Try it yourself. I think you will find that all women at all times have an agenda of leaving men baffled. And, as my resources have noted and as I have more than sufficient evidence to prove, it does work.

I am not drawing on a meager set of resources and experiences for this book. I've had more than my share of contacts with women in my 65 years. I've been around. I've been married twice. I have at least three daughters. I dated five women when I was in high school (unless you count the time I walked my cousin Dorothy to the drugstore for an ice cream cone, in which case you can make that six). I've seen the movies. I was issued a pro kit when I was seventeen years old and serving my time in hell with the Nebraska Air National Guard at summer camp in Casper, Wyoming.

For the purposes of this encyclopedia, I interviewed more than fifteen men about their experiences with women. Okay, actually it was maybe only twelve and it wasn't exactly interviews, more like conversations with my buddies up at the Dannebrog tavern after about six rounds. And they weren't so much talking as they were blubbering and whining, but still, it's not as if I am basing all my conclusions and theories on personal opinion without substantial scientific support.

A Reviewer: A Guy Who's Never Written a Book

Nor is this my first book. A fellow who will remain nameless mostly because he's obviously even more dense than most males posted a review for *Love, Sex, and Tractors* on the Amazon.com Web site that had me mystified. It is generally a positive review:

Where were the tractors?

November 27, 2000

Reviewer: from Richmond, VA, USA

I enjoy reading Mr. Welsch's tractor books, often laughing out loud (and driving my wife crazy). I enjoyed the anecdotes about friends and females, but missed the tractor stories. Maybe it has all been done? I think not. The problems overcome and the lessons learned in *Old Men . . . and Busted Tractors . . .* were rich in both amusement and (some) educational value. This book, unfortunately, left me empty at the end. Funny stories, but a little too much on the "Love and Sex" part; and yet, in some ways, not enough.

The closest this bewildered sap comes to explaining anything at all in his cyber review is his admission that he thinks the book contains too much about love and sex . . . and not enough about love and sex. I think that sums up things rather nicely.

I think this innocent review qualifies as praising with faint damn. But it is also as dumb as a box of rocks. When I write about love and sex, I *am* writing about tractor repair; when I write about tractor repair, I *am* writing about love and sex. The way most men— certainly me—approach these two endeavors, they are pretty much the same.

After reading this confused review I spent the very next day working in the snow, ice, and bitter cold dragging a completely wrecked Allis WC out of the trees where I had parked it years before and muscled it into the shop. Now, please understand, that statement is so casual and unassuming, it defies the logic of language. It's like Alexander the Great starting off his autobiography with "At the age of 23 I had pretty much conquered all of the known world, so I got to thinking about going to cooking school."

Pulling a working tractor on four good wheels with someone riding it and steering, on a pretty, pretty June morning with the birds singing and a belly full of fried potatoes, eggs with just the right amount of hot sauce, and black chicory coffee is a job. But on this occasion I found myself facing a Nebraska winter with an empty shop. Spoiled by three or four perfectly lovely and balmy winters, I had figured about October 1 that I could get a tractor in the shop eventually, sometime when I had plenty of time. Now, well after the first of December, the winter had revealed itself as a howling, bitter, snowy, icy beast, promising to inflict itself on me and mine for many months to come. If I was going to have the comfort of a busted tractor in that shop, it needed to be done in spite of weather, time and personal safety. That was clear.

So I set about doing it. All I have to do is mumble something ever so quietly about moving a tractor and the women and dogs in this household disappear like a brother-in-law when the barmaid brings the tab. So, I would be alone. This means that every couple of feet in the towing process, I have to climb down off the pulling tractor, undo the chain holding the steering on course, adjust the steering wheel (insofar as the ragged snarl of rust and knife blades at the end of the steering column could still be called a steering wheel), rechain it, climb back on the pulling tractor, drag the screaming, lurching hulk a couple feet—and then repeat the whole miserable process.

And that would be after I got the wreck out of the trees. Imagine insofar as you can the scene. All the tires on this tractor are flat and flapping. Two of the wheels are shattered dishes of flaking rust. What isn't broken, is frozen. The temperature is somewhere around 14 degrees. Where the ground is not covered with a couple feet of heavy snow, there is ice. Where there isn't ice, there is the soft sand I was told was rich loam when I bought this place, it was under several feet of snow then, too—a brilliant way to assess and purchase farmland.

The path to the shop is not straight and easy. I have to tow the tractor backwards out from among the trees, around other tractors, onto a road, turn it around, rechain it, and haul it forward another 75 feet to the front of the shop. This takes only, oh, maybe six hours. Amazingly, I wind up bleeding only from some re-opened previous wounds. No new injuries! This may be a record for me!

Once the tractor is situated at right angles to the shop door, maybe thirty feet out from the shop, I unhook the puller tractor and park it handy to the shop so I can repair the front tire that has gone flat while I was doing all this other stuff. Now my task is to turn the tractor wreckage 90 degrees and move it to and into the shop. Without a pulling tractor. Still in the cold, snow, wind, and ice.

Thanks to some clever trading with my buddy, Woodrow, I have a big electric winch anchored in the floor of my shop, at the top of the bay where I work on tractors. This thing is worth its weight in gold. It is old and tired but it gets the job done, which is more than I can say about some of us.

I open the big doors on the shop and drag out the cable and hook it to the front of the tractor. Then I go back into the shop and press the button that starts to turn the tractor and move it slowly, slowly toward the doors. Every couple of feet I again have to go out to the tractor, undo the chain on the steering wheel, readjust the steering, rechain it, walk back into the shop, press the button, move the tractor another few inches. All the while, it's getting colder and colder. Now it's maybe 10 degrees, wind chill maybe 20 below. The wind is picking up. It's spitting just a little snow—or maybe it's sleet.

As the tractor approaches the big doors, I note that the back wheels on this tractor have been turned to the wide setting. I know from experience that this means I will have exactly one inch clearance on each side of those wheels as they come through the door. All that with virtually no steering. If I am more than an inch off, I have to rechain the wreck and pull it back from the shop with the puller tractor and start all over.

The tires are all flat; everything is cold, jammed, stuck, and bent. As the front tires approach the slight incline up to the shop door, the winch says, out loud, "No more!" It has given me its all, but it can't move the wreckage any farther. So, now I dig out a large hand winch, put it onto an anchor in the back of the shop wall, and apply as much pressure as I can, hoping this auxiliary pull will allow the electric winch to drag the wreckage another few inches.

It does. Whew! My options were getting few. Seesawing back and forth between the hand winch and the electric winch, I manage to ease the wreckage through the door and into the shop. But it's not in far enough that I can work around it. This means I will have to jack it up, take off the wheels—which is a labor roughly equivalent to everything I have told you so far—put the tractor on auto dollies, and move it with levers and winches about the shop so I can get around it and under it and still get to my tools and workbench. That process alone will take days of work.

I clean up as much of the mess as I can—chains, cable, pry bars, winches, hammers and screwdrivers (which I use to pry loose stuck chains), hunks of rotten rubber—and I return to the house.

BOTTOM LINE—
THE GUY FROM
VIRGINIA IS STUPID

Pretty ugly, huh? Sounds like a kind of junkyard hell. Well, if that's what you're thinking, you're wrong. It is pure joy. I am tired, filthy, stinky, battered, even a little bloody—and tickled pink. I did it. That's the thing, I did it. The tractor is in that shop. I solved all the problems and set myself up for a winter's worth of fun: dismantling that tractor and fixing it up and making it run, listening to hours of good music, tending to lots of little problems I can fix. There will be surprises, mysteries, warm days in the shop while it snows outdoors, buddies dropping by to talk with me about snags in my repairs, sharing a cold beer and jokes.

So what does this have to do with Mr. Virginia's complaints about my previous book? Everything, that's what. The entire story I told you about wrestling that wrecked tractor into my shop is for all the world the same process we go through every time we take it upon our frail selves to negotiate a relationship with a female human being. At least in Nebraska, if not in Virginia. Switch around a few words in that long description and you have a typical courtship process. My Eastern friend, this is what is called a metaphor, or a parable, (a parable being a metaphor with a moral). The reason your Amazon.com review made no sense to me, or anyone else with the minimum of an ounce of brains and three days experience dealing with a woman, is that it is based on a logical fallacy.

There can't be too little tractor and too much sex and romance in a book about sex and romance because everything in the book about sex and romance is about tractors.

And vice versa. Everything in the book about tractors is about romance and sex. When I wrote in that book about the need for patience, quarts of a good solvent, and a lot of tap-tap-tapping to break loose a stuck bolt, I was talking about love, courtship, romance, and marriage. But I'm trying to put it in terms that make the problems more easily understood by those of us who love and respect good tools, old machinery, a warm shop, a balky engine or a tired transmission. And a cozy bedroom, a woman with a sense of humor but some bad experiences, a reluctant libido but an eagerly responsive body, a tired disposition but a warm heart and open imagination.

More Sex, Less Tractors . . . Or Was It More Tractors, Less Sex?

So, if you are reading along in these pages and get to wondering when I am going to get to more sex, or to more tractors, pause a moment and reconsider. I am talking about relationships when I talk about tractors, and I am talking about tractors when I talk about smooching and hugging. My books, I hope, can be and are enjoyed by everyone. That's my intent. But I am a man, pretty much terminally, and I don't know how to be otherwise. I am comfortable with man stuff, and I tend to talk and write in terms of man stuff. And I tend to do that talking and writing like men tend to talk and write.

I wrote somewhere else how goofy I thought the movie *Something to Talk About* is. Linda and Antonia loved it. It's about relationships. The star is Julia Roberts. My initial complaint about the movie is that I cannot for the life of me imagine making a movie with Julia Roberts and not having her on screen naked as a jaybird at least once, preferable thirty or forty times. It just strikes me as being a good idea. Maybe even common sense. You are paying this woman a mountain of money to make the movie, she is gorgeous beyond belief, so why not ask her to take her clothes off? How complicated can that be?

This incredible artistic error is compounded in that the title telegraphs the story line of the movie, *Something to Talk About*. What the characters in this drama do is talk about it. They talk about everything. Talk talk talk talk talk. Linda and Antonia tell me this is what women do. It is not my impression after considerable observation that this is what men do. Men want to do it, not talk about it, no matter what it is. Eat, sex, uh, something else . . . okay, mostly eat and have sex. My point is still valid. At least I'm pretty sure it's still valid.

Let me reduce this high-flown philosophical abstraction to a solid example, a comparison of two exchanges again from my own experience. The first is a verbatim conversation with my buddy Woodrow, a local plumber:

ME: Hey, Woodrow, our water heater blew up and I need to
           borrow your 24-inch pipe wrench.
WOODROW: Okay.

The second is an exchange between my beloved Linda and me: (Please keep in mind I really do love Linda, Antonia, and women in general. Yes, I want men to enjoy a good and simple life, full of peace and barbecue ribs, but free from the fetters of gender enslavement.)

LINDA: I am wondering if we shouldn't put the box where we throw
        all our old newspapers a little closer to the box where we
        keep our old magazines.
ME: Okay.
LINDA: Because that way when we carry over the slicks and papers,
        we can get rid of them both at the same time.
ME: Okay.
LINDA: See? It would be a lot tidier that way.
ME: Okay.
LINDA: And it would save us trips back and forth with the papers.

ME: Okay.

LINDA: Thus perhaps making it more likely that either you or Antonia will actually pick up after yourselves.

ME: Okay.

LINDA: Since my days seem to be pretty much taken up with following you two around.

ME: Okay.

LINDA: . . . and taking care of things you really could be dealing with yourself . . .

ME: Okay.

LINDA: Instead of pushing the entire load of this miserable household off onto me.

ME: [*Growing increasingly uneasy, looking for an exit, either conversational or physical*] Uh, okay.

LINDA: [*Growing more agitated, slapping a wooden pasta rake into her left hand*] As if I were only a slave around here.

ME: [*Holding up a bolt I happened to spot on the telephone stand, eyeing it with some urgency, as if to suggest that I really need to get this thing out to the shop real quick, for some reason*] Er, yep, right, okay.

LINDA: And not your wife of twenty years . . . twenty years, in fact, this very morning, even though I don't smell any roses or taste any chocolates yet and it's dang near supper time.

ME: [*As door closes behind me and I run barefoot out into the snow*] Oh dear, you spoiled my surprise! Be right back. I have to take this, uh, bolt up to town and pick up the things I bought for you for our, uh, twentieth anniversary . . . twentieth, right? [*Sound of wooden pasta rake hitting door*]

Read this book and think about it, unlike the poor boob who commented on Amazon. Don't write me and say something dumb like "Well, hey, Welscheroo, you told us all about how you deal with your wife, Linda, but my wife's name is Marlene! What am I supposed to do?"

Don't embarrass us, okay? Women are going to read this and they don't need us to hand them any more ammunition. Read a page or two, then do something to encourage your brain juices to flow. Jack Daniels Green Label helps, or staring into the beautiful brown eyes of a black Lab. A day of fishing without too much luck so you have to keep reeling in and rebaiting hooks good. An afternoon reading a good literary essay in a *Playboy* magazine, and then a nappie, that would be good.

And try to think something like, "What does this have to do with women/tractors/children/dogs/roasting ears?" It's all there if you'll just work with me a little bit.

MEN, WOMEN, TRACTORS, SEX

I got into a lot of trouble with the title of *Old Tractors and the Men Who Love Them*. I often get into trouble with titles. My last book was supposed to be *Love, Sex, and Old Tractors: The Eternal Triangle*. See? That's funny. Because love, sex and tractors is not the eternal triangle and therefore still doesn't explain what those three things have to do with each other. Ha-ha-ha-ha-ha-ha! Ha-ha-ha-ha-ha! Ha-ha. Hmmmm. Okay, so it's not comedic genius, but it's better than the way it turned out.

On the other hand, I have no one to blame for *Old Tractors and the Men Who Love Them* but myself. Thing is, the stereotype of the tractor mechanic as a male—even an old-goat male like me—raised some hackles on some very pretty and delicate female necks. Okay, there are women out there who work on tractors too. And kids. The gender, personality, age, religion, and peanut butter preference of people who love tractors can't be pinned down that easily.

The thing is, I'm an old fart who likes tractors and so are most of the guys I pal around with. And for that matter, most of the people who read my stuff. Yes, I know the rest of you are out there, and hopefully you enjoy my stuff too—but well, you know. Now, this book is *not* about tractors. It's about women. Okay, and about tractors insofar as women are like tractors. I know there are all sorts of exceptions out there to everything I say here about men, women, and damn near everything else. I have plenty of evidence that says that my experience with a lot of things, especially women and tractors, is the experience of an awful lot of other people too.

I have had run-ins with thoroughly evil, nasty, ugly, hateful women—and with a lot more who are dreams and delights. I don't hate women, far from it. I delight in them. I adore my wife, daughters, and mother, and lots of other women too. I genuinely and thoroughly enjoy women.

So keep a couple things in mind as you read these pages: First, Lovely Linda has read this book, laughed at it, and said that she learned a lot about men, and me, from it, and thinks it is a contribution to each gender's understanding of the other. I sure hope so.

Second, for Pete's sake, the book is supposed to be funny! In the editorial process this book has passed through the hands and under the eyes of more women than men. They all have understood my dirty little secret: This book is not about women. It's about men. And I am laughing at my gendermates, because we're laughable, but we're also adorable. As Lovely Linda so often says to me, "Welsch, it's a good thing you're so darn cute." So, lighten up. If you read this and think I'm picking on women, you're reading it wrong. Start over, and do it right.

CHAPTER 2

THE LANGUAGE
OF LOVE

Do you not know I am a woman?
When I think, I must speak.

—SHAKESPEARE, *AS YOU LIKE IT*

My training and experience is in anthropology. That's how I came to have such an interest in and spent so much energy studying the most exotic human form of all: woman. Important to any anthropological study is language, and the lessons we find in language can be instructive beyond mere communications.

When I was an undergraduate doing linguistic research, I spent many Saturdays working with the language of the Omaha Indians. One of the first lessons I learned from my resource person, Clyde Sheridan, was that I should be careful when learning vocabulary to note that in the Omaha tribe, women speak a different language than men.

I could accept that. After all, even at the tender age of twenty I knew that men and women speak a different language. Men, for example, use the expression *"right away"* as in "Yes, dear, I'll take care of the faucet drip *right away*," to mean "eventually," "in good time," "when I get around to it," "as soon as this game is over, or maybe tomorrow when that game is over." Women, on the other hand, use "right away" to mean either "right away" as in "immediately," or "never" as in "Yeah, I'll arrange a three-way with my best friend and us *right* away."

In the Omaha language, men and women actually use differ-ent words for the same thing. Actually that's not even all that unusual. When I was a lad, my dad taught me that horses sweat, men perspire, and women glow, for example. And Mom made it clear that while men fart, women fluff. Not that women ever do that, of course.

If you are a man over ten years of age, you have almost certainly experienced this language differential. Your mother says, "If you ever do that again, darling, I'm going to slap you thirty ways from Tuesday." What exactly does the word "darling" mean in that context? It means "Stupid." This word has been used in this way on several occasions during our marriage. For example, the time(s) I have tracked dog poop into the kitchen, or dribbled fish juice through the living room, or turned all the laundry a kind of neutral grayish lilac. You know, the kinds of things every man does at some time or another, in total innocence, with nothing but good intentions.

Linda has said, "Welsch, it's a good thing you're so cute." But I can pretty much tell by her inflection on the word "cute" that she's not using it in quite the way I would use it, for example, to describe Pamela Anderson's behind. For Linda, it seems to connote something more along the line of Mr. Ed's behind.

EXAMPLES OF LINGUISTIC DYSPHASIA

For all practical purposes, men and women speak two entirely different languages. We may even use the same words, but somehow the meanings are lost. This is not a goofy notion of mine, not a unique discovery. All men know it, and probably some women, although I don't know about them. I don't speak their language, after all.

To give you some idea of previous treatments of this problem, allow me to provide you with this sample from a seventy-year-old movie, *It's a Gift*, starring something of an expert in human nature, and certainly of the nature of the females species, W.C. Fields.

W.C. FIELDS: [*In bed with his wife, the phone rings, he answers*] Hello, hello. No, no, this isn't the maternity hospital. [*Hangs up and gets back into bed*]

WIFE: Who was it?

W.C.: Somebody called up and wanted to know if this is the maternity hospital.

WIFE: What did you tell them?

W.C.: I told them no, it wasn't the maternity hospital.

WIFE: Funny thing they should call *you* here at this hour of the night . . . from the *maternity* hospital.

W.C.: They didn't call *me* up *here*, from the maternity hospital. They wanted to know if this *was* the maternity hospital.

WIFE: Oh, so now you're *changing* it.

W.C.: No, I didn't change it, dear. I told you, they asked me if this was the maternity hospital . . .

WIFE: [*Interrupting*] Don't . . . oh, don't make it any worse.

Why am I bothering to give you that example? You've been there if you've ever spent more than fifteen minutes with a woman. You've heard it from others if you haven't. But of course you understand the humor of the scene. What's funny is that no matter what Fields did following this point in the conversation, he was going to make it worse. By being alive, he made it worse. Even if he'd been dead, he would have made it worse. No matter what, it got worse.

The W.C. Fields dialogue is funny because it is ethnologically accurate. Most men can recite a virtually identical conversation from their own experience—probably from their *recent* experience. I recall once dining at my parents' home with my first wife. My mother asked if I would like some Brussels sprouts. Before I could respond, my wife-at-the-time said, "Roger doesn't like Brussels sprouts." I was astonished. Because I love Brussels sprouts. I said, logically I thought, "But, I *like* Brussels sprouts!"

Equally logically, but within a different logic system, Wife #1 said firmly, "Well, I'm glad you've changed your mind."

I LOVE YOU—MEANING . . .

This cross-gender linguistic confusion works both ways. Just as women use words differently from men, so men use words differently from women. Women say "I love you," meaning, "From now on the assumption will be that you don't so much as look at another woman, much less talk with her. Your binges up at the tavern with your hunting buddies are now at an end. You'll have to get rid of that motorcycle, and the dog. You will be allowed one cigar a year, burned outdoors, thank you. I hereby accept your tacit agreement to follow my every order, and react to instant changes in those decisions, even if they constitute a 180-degree reversal. I also accept your willingness to do whatever things I tell you to do, even if they offend millions of years of male pride in such things as facial hair, eating raw meat, or really superfast lovemaking. From now on you will be expected to remember each and every anniversary in our relationship, no matter how trivial, and to buy me expensive presents for all of them, because that's what I want. And, by the way, I go crazy for a week or so every month."

When a man says, "I love you" it means something like, "You don't by any chance know how to make mashed potatoes, do you?"

It's not as if men are bad at language and women are good at it. We are both inarticulate stutterers, and the result is inevitably a linguistic dead end. But men do seem to miss more dramatically the implications of communication. A couple evenings ago my buddy, Woodrow, a pretty savvy guy all in all, was up in the tavern having himself a good time. That is only a guess on my part because I wasn't there. In fact, everything in the scenario I'm about to tell you is a guess, but I know Woodrow, and I know men, and I know how these things go.

BEER POISONING

My only clue was a phone call, from the tavern—not from Woodrow. Somewhere in his premium-malt-and-fine-hops genius (the next day he told me he had suffered momentary "beer poisoning") he made a typically male communications decision. Here's the way I'm guessing his reasoning went: "I'm having one good time here and because it's only two hours after Rog's bed time [8:00 P.M.], I think I'll call him and invite him to come up here for a couple beers. But, I'll bet Linda is somewhere there around the phone too, so I better think about this.

"Okay. If *I* call, she's going to think, 'That no-good Woodrow is going to get Rog up there and fill him full of beer and then I'll never get him to mow the lawn tomorrow,' so *I* won't call. Maybe I'll have *Lunchbox* call. No, then Linda would think, 'That no-good Lunchbox is going to get Rog up there and fill him full of beer and then I'll never get him to clean off the back porch tomorrow,' so I won't have *Lunchbox* call. So, maybe I'll have Melvin call and . . . no . . . maybe Bruce . . . no . . . Hey! I got it! I'll have Tiffany, the barmaid who also dances on the table when she is feeling good and dresses provocatively and runs the karaoke make the call. Yeah, that would be a good idea."

And that's what he did. He had Tiffany call and laugh and giggle into our answering machine that she was wondering if maybe Rogie couldn't come out and play. Oh yeah. Right. You bet. Linda's going to go for that! Now, I'll be lucky if I can so much as go in that place to buy root beer for the next six years.

Another place where the Omaha tribe seemed to have a much better grasp on the realities of male-female relationships than we do was within what we would call in-law relationships. Don't get me wrong. I truly do love my mother-in-law, Sally. She's a prize, but I hear from my extensive contacts with the outside world that this is not always the way things go. Within the Omaha tribe, *any* communications between a man and a woman who could potentially be his mother-in-law (that is, any woman with a marriageable daughter) was forbidden. How's that for ethnological good sense?

A ROSE BY ANY OTHER NAME

There is a belief in many cultures that words have a force and power within themselves. Merely mentioning the name of something can influence it or cause it to appear. Which, in a lot of situations, is not a good idea. It is not wise, for example, to tempt such an appearance by, say, Satan. Thus, "Speak of the devil . . . " when someone shows up right after you mention his name. The only large, dangerous animal in historical Europe was the bear, and you didn't want one of those things showing up. So you played it safe by referring to that creature only as "bruin," or "the brown one." Just playing it safe.

That's why we call God "God," a kind of generic description, not a name at all. Thing is, you never know what happens when you invite God to a party, so maybe it's best just not to mention His name at all. That way, maybe He won't notice. It's with this same kind of awe and fear, it has been speculated, that men pretty much universally refer to their wives as "Sweetie," "Love," "Dear," "Honeybunch," or "Love Cakes"—disgusting labels like these that no self-respecting man should ever actually say out loud.

There are other reasons for such usage, I have been advised. Not long ago a joke circulated around here about rodeo sex. If you asked the speaker what rodeo sex could possibly be, he would respond that you engage your wife in connubial intercourse and about the time things get to going really well, you call her by your last girlfriend's name. And then see if you can hang on for seven seconds.

Calling your wife by another woman's name at any time is dangerous business, but some times are definitely worse than others. I know men who would date only women named Betty or Ann to avoid just such a gaffe. Another, easier solution is simply never to refer to the woman in your life by her name, but only by "Sweetie," "Love," "Dear," "Honeybunch," "Love Cakes." Things start to fall into place now, don't they?

The whole issue of love names is a delicate balance. I like it when Linda calls me "Rog." That's nice. Sort of neutral, modestly affectionate. "Roger Lee Welsch" is not good. Something is wrong when she calls me "Roger Welsch," and there is rarely much doubt who is responsible. "Sweetie," "Love," "Dear," "Honeybunch," or "Love Cakes" are not much better. When she uses lovey terms like that, it suggests a major hemorrhage in our checking account, a dent in the car, or fish cakes for supper.

My problem here, almost certainly, is that there is a major difference in how men and women use nicknames. My pals include Dan, Dennis, John, Eric, Mick, Dick, and Dave. I refer to them familiarly as Slack Time, Lunchbox, Boomer, Slick, Mick the Brick, Dickie Doodles, and Mojo. If we're really having a good time and have downed a couple beers, they may be variously addressed as Fart Breath, Shit for Brains, Clabber Ass, Wienie, Easy Money, or Dick (but not the guy named Dick, of course).

Women who may read this won't believe it but any man knows it's true. If some guy no one likes comes into a group setting then it really gets ugly; nobody calls him anything. It is really painful to watch. Poor guy. No one likes him well enough to insult him. It's enough to make you weep.

Linda's friends are Lisa, Ann, Kay, Josephine, and Stephanie. It is not my impression that she refers to them as anything but Lisa, Ann, Kay, Josephine, and Stephanie. Because it has taken me more than fifty years to uncover the whole secret of Woman School, it is possible that during those long breaks to the ladies room in the tavern or while they are shopping at Kmart or when taking in a movie, they push each other around by the shoulder and call themselves Lard Butt, Training Bra, Stinky, and Easy. I just don't know. But that's not my impression. Let me know if you find out anything different.

WHEN WORDS FAIL

Within our own, Western, Anglo-American, mainstream culture, women and men exchange words but rarely communicate with each other. For example, I once ran across the fascinating information in my reading that Ladhra, one of the leaders of Ireland's legendary early six races, had sixteen wives and reportedly died of an excess of women.

When I passed this tidbit of anthropological information along to Linda, she commented snippily, "A lesson for all philanderers." My own interpretation was that it shouldn't take nearly that many wives to constitute an excess. See? Same verbal input—but with very different conclusions being drawn. I should also note a difference in linguistic delivery systems between the genders: Linda said her retort quietly but aloud. Me, I just pretty much kept my wise-ass remark to myself, it being only an hour or so to suppertime and the smells from the kitchen suggesting that digestion is the better part of valor.

Contrary to belief and Woman School teachings, one simply cannot assume that the pure, innocent, sweet, and chaste interpretation of texts and/or a word will be the distaff product while the lecherous, obscene, suggestive, lewd slant is necessarily masculine. Yes, that does seem to be generally the case. There is simply no way in billy-hell that a woman is going to drive into a service station with a sputtering car and say to a man, "Could you take a look under my hood? I think my whatchamacallit is stuck," and have that man not have at least a scintilla of a temptation to say something like, "Your place or mine?" Just ain't gonna happen.

AS USUAL, WOMEN KNOW THIS, MEN DON'T

Nor is such a straight line any more an accident than the resulting *double-entendre* is a coincidence. I have been told about a lovely young lady, capable of a studied and deliberate outward appearance that absolutely *glowed* with innocence, who would occasionally, on a whim, launch off into a story about the time she was "rear-ended in a parking lot" and how "totally scrunched her bumpers were" simply to watch the boy in the shipping room turn fiery red, sputter and stammer, and run to wash his face under the water cooler. She knew exactly what she was doing to this pathetic boob with her quasi-erotic story, and she loved repeating the process just to watch him squirm.

Anyway, this may be an old story, but it happened to me just as I am about to tell you. It makes my point that sometimes the innocence of the matter falls to the male, while the gleeful leer literally leaps from the driven snow, as it were. I dropped in at our town tavern just to check the time (okay, maybe *that* part of the story isn't true, but the rest of it is). And there was a familiar local sitting at the bar, looking for all the world like a tomcat fresh out of the clothes dryer. I sat down beside him, ordered a draw, and asked him why he seemed so frazzled. The following is *exactly* what he told me.

"Well, Rog, to tell you the truth, I'm not even sure what happened to me today. You know that black mare I've been trying to sell for a while now? Well, this morning this guy offers me five hundred dollars for that mare, which is a fair, even good price. So I said sure. But then he gets to bargaining and says he wants a fifteen percent discount for paying cash.

"Well, Rog, I'm not too good at cipherin', so I sat there with a scratch pad trying to figure out fifteen percent of five hundred dollars and was getting nowhere fast, so I excused myself and high tailed it over to the schoolteacher's house on Sycamore Street. I knocked at her door and she answered and I says, 'Now, if I was to offer you five hundred dollars for something but wanted a fifteen percent discount for paying cash, how much would you take off?' So help me, Rog, she says just like that, 'Everything but my socks and earrings.'"

See? Men and women say the same things with the same words, in contrast to the more open and obvious Omaha language where they have the common sense to use different vocabularies, but somehow the meanings carried to each gender are not the same. I think of a time when we were just building this house of ours and I got one of my first hints that Antonia, even at the tender age of four, was already getting basic lessons in Woman School.

A bunch of us were standing around in the new basement talking with our contractor and good friend, Mick, when a mouse ran out of one of the piles of rubble and made a dash across the new floor. Our dog, Slump, took a mighty and courageous leap and landed on that poor unfortunate mouse. Well, it was a pretty ugly scene for Linda and Antonia, so Mick and I pulled Slump away, and there lay this poor maimed mouse. Linda said something like, "Rog, can you do something about that?" and I said, "Yeah, I'll take care of it." I picked up the wounded mouse and headed for the door.

To my amazement, Antonia, just a tot, said, "Can I go with you, Dad?"

Well, I had chosen to move out to this farm, in part to show Antonia what life is all about, and I guess dispatching a fatally injured mouse is one of those grand lessons. So, yeah, she could come along. We went outside, where I put the mouse on the ground and stepped on it to give it a merciful departure.

Antonia gasped, "Well, that's not what *I* call 'taking care of it!'"

Whoops! "To take care of" has two different meanings. To this male, it meant provide a merciful end to the suffering. To the female (even the four-year-old female) it meant "to tend to, care for, bandage up, and serve hot tea."

The linguistic confusion between the genders doesn't end, ever, no matter how old we get. Just a few days ago I was watching the fetching Condoleezza Rice on a television talk show, doing her best to explain away yet another Bush boneheadism and I said to no one in particular, "I wonder if that woman ever asks herself how she got tied up with that sorry boob." From the kitchen came a mumbled response from Linda, "Rog, sooner or later every married woman asks herself that same question."

See? What I said was perfectly logical and straightforward, and still Linda didn't get my point.

LANGUAGE REFLECTS CULTURE

We all know that language reflects culture. Even if you never took a college anthropology course, you know the old story about Eskimos having a slew of words for different kinds of snow, because snow in its various conditions is so critical to Arctic life, while Polynesian fishing peoples have similarly rich vocabularies for ocean conditions, and types of fish. American men have all kinds of words exclusive to their gender for objects and processes important to them. Pork rind textures, fishing bobber types, barbecue charcoal ignition, dog breath, smut . . .

Women are: 1) oblivious to those linguistic niceties and 2) privy to their *own* gender-specific vocabulary. Lipstick colors, parallel parking techniques, and what all that stuff is in a purse.

Understandably, there is plenty of room here for miscommunication. In fact, the miracle is when any understanding whatsoever is arrived at between a man and a woman. Not only do we not use the same words, we don't even use the same logic systems.

Not long ago my daughter Antonia was about to go to Lincoln for something or another, and I suggested that maybe a couple friends of mine could help her make her way around town, give her a place to stay overnight, maybe even have some fun with her while she was there.

Linda had expressed considerable concern about the situation. Would this couple have a bedroom ready for her? Would they be able to help her around this town with which she wasn't familiar? Would the short notice be a problem? Would they be able to make connections? Could they get Antonia to her bus and on her way home the next day? Did they perhaps already have plans for the weekend? Were they prepared to handle hosting a teenager in their home where there were no other children of any age?

Well, how complicated can it be? I figured I'd just call Joyce and set things up. I should have known it wasn't going to be that simple. I called, but the lady of the house wasn't at home. Well, okay—I figured I'd just clear everything with the man of the house. And that's what we did:

ME: Hey, buddy, Antonia is coming to Lincoln tomorrow and I'm wondering if she can stay with you guys.
MALE FRIEND: Sure.
ME: Can you also pick her up at the coliseum on Friday evening?
MALE FRIEND: Yeah.
ME: Great. And then take her back out there on Saturday evening?
MALE FRIEND: No problem.
ME: Thanks, buddy. See you soon.
MALE FRIEND: Okay, Rog. Thanks for calling.

At that point I figured everything had been taken care of. In fact, I was rather proud of myself for having taken care of all the details. Linda likes, after all, to make a point about how men don't pay attention to details while, of course, women do. Well, ha, ha, and double ha! My male friend and I certainly did set that myth to rest, I hoped, once and for all.

At this point the drama splits and explodes, taking place on two different stages at precisely the same time, a fact that I discovered only later in my research. At my home, proud of how well I had handled this, I went up to Linda's office to accept her compliments and gratitude:

ME: Hey, hon . . . that problem with Antonia going to Lincoln? I took care of it.

LINDA: Oh my God, no! What have you done?

ME: Uh, well, I just called my friend and made arrangements. Antonia can stay with him and his wife. He'll see that she gets to where she needs to go when she needs to be there.

LINDA: You didn't talk with his wife . . .

ME: [*Sensing that a major omission is about to be discussed*] Uuuuh . . . I think I have some things I really need to do out in the shop . . . .

What I didn't know was that a similar conversation was taking place at the other end, at my friends' home. The woman came home and the following conversation ensued with her husband, as I later found out in a post-disaster debriefing:

MALE FRIEND: Rog called and Antonia is coming to spend the weekend.

FEMALE FRIEND: *This* weekend? Like, *tomorrow*? We don't even have the spare bed put together! And the upstairs bathroom isn't working yet. We just moved in Wednesday . . . and you are taking in houseguests on Friday?

MALE FRIEND: Uh . . .

FEMALE FRIEND: Did she say what time she's coming?

MALE FRIEND: Well, uh, no, not exactly.

FEMALE FRIEND: Or where you're supposed to pick her up?

MALE FRIEND: [*With new found confidence*] Yes, she did. I'm picking her up at the coliseum.

FEMALE FRIEND: Which gate? The coliseum is huge! Do you even know where the coliseum is?

MALE FRIEND: I think I have something I really need to do in the basement.

The next time we got together as couples, the two women, clicked their tongues and shook their heads and sniffed in our direction. Her husband and I did a high-five about what a grand job we had done. Everything worked out just fine, after all. Then we drank a mess of beer and had a contest to see who could belch the loudest.

(Our female friend later told us that actually she is prepared for such events because now and again the clunk in her life—that's what she called him, "the clunk in my life"—will get a phone call from some of his buddies. There is mention of a big ball game and out of the blue, this idiot invites four guys to come over and spend the evening watching TV and drinking beer. Immediately upon hanging up, he turns to her and says that he has to run over to the Qwik Stop and pick up some beer and potato chips. Maybe she could entertain his friends until he gets back, and move the laundry down to the end of the couch.)

My wife and his made primal noises of agreement, looked contemptuously at the two of us, and did The Sigh.

THE SIGH

All men know about The Look. It was the great American ethnologist Jerry Seinfeld who presented the definitive study of The Look. He didn't invent The Look, nor did he discover it. Every man alive, if he has had one instant of time with a woman daughter, mother, wife, grocery store clerk, woman sitting in her car at a stoplight at whom you glanced while wondering what she might look like naked, *knows* The Look. Seinfeld simply put together an episode of his television sitcom that gave the widespread phenomenon a name and provided a series of examples for The Look.

It is my pleasure, privilege, and responsibility to do the same for The Sigh. If the next few paragraphs, considered along with my exposing of Woman School and composing the Male Generic Apology, don't win me both a Pulitzer Prize for Literature and a Nobel Peace Prize, I just don't know what the heck literature and peace are supposed to be all about.

As with The Look, every man living and dead has experienced The Sigh. Women learn The Sigh early in Woman School. You can see little moppets on the playground at your local school perform The Sigh. A little boy has the incredible good luck of finding a dung beetle, complete with the cute little ball of poop he is busily rolling off to charm some dung beetle lady, and the kid has put the beetle in an Altoids tin to bring to school to impress the young ladies in *his* life.

Are they impressed? (The girls, not the lady dung beetles, who probably *are* impressed because bugs tend to be more logical and reasonable than human females.) No, they are not. First they are disgusted, then they are mad, and then they heave The Sigh, which pretty much finishes off any further discussion.

THE SIGH IN ACTION

It simply does not matter who is right or wrong in a discussion where The Sigh is brought into play. The Sigh is the ultimate trump, the H-bomb of domestic litigation. Once again let me provide you with a real-life dialogue.

FEMALE: This is curious. These guys on television are talking about the D-day landing on Omaha Beach. Why would we have invaded Omaha at a time when there wasn't much more there than the stockyards?

MALE: It wasn't Omaha, Nebraska. It was Omaha Beach—just across the English Channel from England, in France.

FEMALE: Don't be silly. Omaha is in Nebraska. It's an Indian word, for Pete's sake. Why would Indians be in France? You're such a silly.

MALE: They just called the landing area Omaha.

FEMALE: Why?

MALE: Because they needed to call it something.

FEMALE: If the French want to call something something, they call it a French something. It's illegal to use American words, let alone American *Indian* words in France. The point is, why would we invade Omaha, Nebraska?

MALE: It was *not* Omaha, Nebraska. It was Omaha *Beach*, in France. I know what I'm talking about. You weren't even born on D-day, and I was already buying war stamps and hauling copper to school for scrap drives, so believe me, I am right on this one. If you don't believe me, look it up in the blasted encyclopedia. See? Here it is: Omaha *Beach . . . in FRANCE . . . on D-day!*

FEMALE: [Pauses, narrows eyes, cocks head slightly to one side, and gives The Sigh!]

That doesn't mean you were wrong, and in fact the woman in question here may actually be admitting in a very subtle way that you were right. But by heaving The Sigh into the mix, she is pretty much closing the book on this particular discussion. While you may indeed be correct, she is saying that your attitude, lack of diplomacy, the tone of your voice, your inability to sort laundry correctly, and that damn ever-open toilet lid has earned you The Sigh. So shut up, give up, and just do a crossword puzzle or something.

THE TONE

Now we are really getting technical. If you are a male over twelve, you have almost certainly heard The Tone. You are having an argument—no, let's say you are only having a *discussion* with a woman. Nothing important, something you are fairly certain about, and the issue seems to be pretty much settled. Let me provide you with an example from my own experience.

LINDA: What's this word on my shopping list?

ME: Marmalade. I would like some orange marmalade.

LINDA: I'll look for some for you.

ME: Thank you.

LINDA: But it's spelled m-a-r-m-A-l-a-d-e. Three a's, only one e. At the end. Marmalade.

ME: Actually, I'm pretty sure it's m-a-r-m-E-l-a-d-e. Of course you could be right. Main thing is, I'd like some.

At this point her voice takes on The Tone. The difficulty here is that in print it looks as if she is agreeing with me. But if you read the following words in italics out loud and at the same time drag two pieces of glass across each other, you can come kinda close to the reality.

LINDA: Okay, *Mr. College English Professor*, I suppose you're right. You're the educated one in the family. Okay, instead of getting you *marmAHlade* then, I'll get you some *marmEHlade*.

And she will. Later that same day I will find two jars of exactly what I want on the shelf in the kitchen. With a huge Magic Marker circle around that little bitsy "a" sticking out of the damn word "marmalade" like a dead fly in a big tureen of blue cheese dressing. Still alive and swimming.

THE SHRUG

The Shrug may be used alone or in combination with any of the other feminine rhetorical nuclear devices discussed in these pages. As with The Tone, the words you hear sound for all the world like she has caved in and now agrees with you. You have won. She has surrendered. The discussion is over. But not quite. Even after The Tone and The Sigh have faded, there is still ample opportunity for The Shrug.

Everything has been said, everything is settled, and then with a little wrinkle of the edge of her mouth, one shoulder almost imperceptibly lifted in a flash higher than the other, a swivel on a heel, and a cute butt swish, everything that has gone before is erased. It's gone—all the reasoning, all the arguments, all the proofs, all the evidence—gone. Nothing you said mattered. It's like leading in a football game forty-six to zero for fifty-nine and a half minutes and then, somehow, with the last thirty seconds on the scoreboard, the other team inexplicably scores six touchdowns, a field goal, and—oh God!—a safety and the game is over. That's how The Shrug works. Don't even look at the scoreboard, check the tapes, or ask for a rematch. You lost.

A CONVERSATION ABOUT CONVERSATION

I happen to believe that not only are the gender vocabularies different, and the intonation, and the syntax, but the very notions of the two species of what communication are vastly different from each other. Just last night I observed an example. My old buddy Mick the Brick is coming out sometime today to help me haul my annual mess of hams—40 of them, about a third of a ton's worth—out of the curing brine, onto my truck, down to the smokehouse, and up on the racks. We talked about this earlier in the week and he said he'd be here. I said that afternoon would be about right. He could stay over and in the morning we could work the smudge again.

The conversation took about five minutes and when we finished it up, neither of us could think of any more questions. This morning Linda and I had a conversation about yesterday's conversation, it took about an hour and was nothing but questions:

LINDA: What time is Mick going to be here?

ME: Sometime today.

LINDA: Well, okay, but what *time*?

ME: This afternoon, maybe late.

LINDA: What *time*?

ME: [*Guessing*] 3:16.

LINDA: Is he staying over?

ME: [*Triumphant because I have an answer*] YES!

LINDA: One night?

ME: [*Re-bewildered*] Uuuuuuuh . . . ..

LINDA: Are you planning on supper here?

ME: [*Confusion deepening*] I . . . uh . . .

LINDA: Are you staying here or at the cabin?

ME: [*Exploring my pockets for something sharp I might be able to use to slit my wrists*]: Uh?

LINDA: Do you think he's still coming?

At this point I broke off the conversation with my own version of The Shrug, The Sigh, and The Look. Of course he is coming! Didn't he *say* he's coming? Wasn't our clear understanding that he would be coming? Isn't it fairly well determined that he will be here? I think so, and that means that Mick the Brick *will* be here.

Or maybe not.

THE CURSE

I can't get through this chapter without discussing cussing. I have known women who can blister the paint off of farm machinery with their vocabulary, but I think generally women can accomplish without cussing what men more often than not need ten or fifteen large-caliber obscenities to do. Linda hardly ever cusses. Which, of course, lends a very special quality to what she has to say when she does cuss. But mostly, she doesn't cuss.

In fact, when we first got together twenty years ago, in her most furious moments, when her bile reached the boiling point and her anger was utterly irrepressible, she would mutter, "Dad gum it." (No exclamation point. She was never *that* mad.) Then I pointed out to her that "dad gum it" is a spooneristic euphemism: a traditional way to soften a tough term by simply changing around the initial sounds of its words. In this case, changing "goddam it" to "dad gum it." She never used the phrase again. And in fact, being a woman with advanced degrees from Woman School, she insists she never did use it. I provide examples, transcripts, audiotapes, and witnesses; she sighs; I lose the argument.

Thing is, Linda doesn't need tough language. Whatever she says in anger is given death-ray potency by the *way* she says it. For example, a couple weeks ago my big, dumb-but-goodhearted black Lab, Thud, jumped up in glee about something or another. He does that, smacking Linda in the nose and inflicting considerable pain. It was only an angry reaction, one I'm sure she later regretted, but within that instant her pain and surprise brought her to the threshold of common decency and she exploded in fury. She stood there holding her injured nose and shocked both me and Thud (it took her almost three days to get the two of us out from under the back porch) by muttering in Thud's direction, "You . . . you . . . you idiot-head." I'm not exaggerating here. Ask Linda herself. She called Thud an idiot-head.

On one hand, both Thud and I blinked our eyes in confusion because, well, shouldn't an occasion like this call for something more authentic and substantial in the way of insult and anger? I mean, jeez. But then the real horror of the situation swept over the two of us like a tsunami: she called him an idiot-head! The sky went dark. Life as we knew it ended.

After the initial shock and fear, I mostly felt sorry for poor ol' Thud. And I prayed 24 hours straight, to all that is sacred to me and some gods I never believed in before, that she never gets angry enough to call *me* an idiot-head! Yikes, yikes, and double yikes. Idiot-head.

Whew. Poor Thud's never been the same. Neither have I.

THE SCREAM

The Scream in the full and terrifying sense of that word and device is not often used by women. There are roller coaster screams, and anger screams, and even screams of delight (some so disconcerting they have left men utterly impotent the rest of their lives), but The Scream—capital T, capital S—is a rare phenomenon. And it's a good thing. I have heard The Scream once in my life. It was Linda. I was downstairs, she was up in our bedroom. I heard The Scream.

> *Women are wiser than men because they know less and understand more.*
> —JAMES STEPHENS,
> *THE CROCK OF GOLD*

About a half hour later the dogs and I came back to the farm, crawling up from behind trees and bushes, still trembling, still a little embarrassed about the fact that we had wet ourselves. I came back into the house through the back door, which I had pretty much demolished in my haste to get out only moments earlier. There was Linda, still hopping up and down, biting the knuckles of her left hand, terror in her eyes. She had been sorting laundry in the bedroom and across the floor had run—a mouse. And she screamed The Scream.

She grimaced that I *had* to go upstairs and take care of that mouse. Okay, sure. But if a grown man and three black labs had fled the scene, didn't it also seem likely that the mouse, who was so much closer to the blast area, might also have gone his way? No matter. I had to go upstairs and look for the mouse. Reassured that the sound I'd heard wasn't Gabriel's Horn, I went up the stairs, prepared to make whatever perfunctory noises needed to convince her that I'd done my manly duty.

I looked around quickly, as futile as that seemed to be, and there—good grief! Lying on the floor in plain sight, nothing of substance even close to him, nothing that might have hit him, or that the sonic blast might have hurled him into, was that mouse. Belly up, dead as, well, dead as a dormouse. There were no signs of injury on him other than a little blood from each tiny ear and a look of indescribable horror on his face. I'm not kidding you here: Linda's Scream had killed him right where he stood.

God only knows what The Scream could do to you or me, Brother Male. I don't think we want to know.

THE TEAR

Almost as devastating but apparently only on men (not on mice), is The Tear. I'm not going to spend a lot of time or space on this issue because if I give more than a moment's thought to a tear on the cheek of Linda, Antonia, Mom, Joyce, Jenny, or Jacinda, I'll have to run out and buy about a billion dollars worth of roses and chocolates and make promises about Caribbean cruises, new cars, and endless hours of conversation about relationships. I certainly don't want to do that. Besides, if you are a man, you probably already know more about The Tear than you want to.

THE WHAMMY

There are ancient and generally discounted beliefs about the importance of women not being around baking bread or brewing beer during, well, you know, during . . . *that* time of the month.

The notion is that the mere presence of a menstruating woman in the same room can fritz processing bread or beer. Ha-ha-ha-ha. Well, no one these days believes in that kind of foolish superstition. However, like so many ancient beliefs that are discounted by the oh-so scientific and modern, there is increasing evidence that this may be founded, like most folk wisdom, in empirical evidence. People saw enough failed bread and wine spoiled by the presence of women, especially at certain times in their, uh, months, that someone commented on it. Others found that was their experience too, they decided to avoid spoiled bread and wine, and so the belief was born.

> *A man is always wrong,*
> *even when he's right.*
> —GEORGE SCHWELLE,
> SCHWELLE'S RULES
> OF ORDURE

Modern research suggests that enzymes secreted dermally by women during certain points of their cycle inhibit yeast growth, the heart of successful bread- and wine-making. I know that some women consider that kind of information an insult. Not because it is wrong, I suspect, but because someone, i.e., a male, has figured it out. But there it is and you can deny it all you want, but if it is indeed the truth, maybe it's worth keeping in mind.

I'm almost afraid to tell you this item of information it is so creepy. Moreover, I don't know if it is just Linda or if women in general are born with this or if it is part of the standard Woman School curriculum.

You may think I'm nuts, and maybe I am, but what I am about to tell you is also absolutely true. There may be a logical, scientific explanation or it may be voodoo and witchcraft. I don't know, but this is truly the way it happened.

The first time I realized the full depth of her powers, Linda was driving and we were on a highway not far from our home when some idiot-adolescent went roaring around us, on a curve, at well over the speed limit, a real hazard to anyone else on the highway. Linda muttered something completely understandable about how she wished someone like that would have his car engine blow up so he could sit alongside the highway and watch us go by at a civilized and legal pace. Then she got this funny look in her eye. At that very instant, a puff of oil smoke billowed out from under that speeding car and it limped totally disabled and smoking to the shoulder of the road. Where it sat as we passed by, smiling at a civilized and legal pace.

Another day some time later: Linda is driving again. This time we are on a four-lane highway, proceeding at a little less than the speed limit. A large truck of trash goes by us, spewing branches, leaves, twigs, brush into the air, over the side, onto the road, and into the ditch. Linda, in her gentle way comments on how dreadful it is that this jerk is so carelessly messing up the highway and posing a real hazard to anyone behind him, not to mention going way too fast. Then there is that look, about the moment I watch the truck with riveted attention waiting for the engine to blow up, the engine blows up. Again, billows of blue smoke, dreadful noises of an engine self-destructing, and that slow, painful roll over to the shoulder of the road.

I don't recall that I said much at that time. Mostly I was thinking of the times I might have made Linda mad and what she said at the time. I looked at her in stunned amazement. The conclusion is now unavoidable: Linda can blow up internal-combustion engines from a distance of a quarter mile or so.

How many men, I wonder, have been driving along ten or twelve miles above the speed limit, not noticing the tin cans blowing out of the truck bed, maybe giving some special admiration to a lovely young woman driving along in her passenger car, maybe shooting pheasants while still moving at seventy miles an hour when the engine suddenly blows up for no reason at all? And how many men just cursed their luck and sat there for an hour waiting for some other buddy to come get them and bring fresh beer, or maybe tried to explain their condition to a state trooper, never for a moment imagining that some woman like Linda used a magical mental zapper to blow up their engine? Not me. I know what happened to that engine.

What other mystic arrows are there in the female quiver? I have no idea but I'm not about to go out of my way to make myself a target. You can count on that.

NOTE FROM SERIES EDITOR

We here at Man School Publications realize that this is only a preliminary inventory of the linguistic and psychic devices taught and practiced at Woman School. Our research division is constantly at work collecting and analyzing other female phenomena. In future annual updates of this encyclopedia we will make our results available to male subscribers. Currently underway are projects investigating what women mean when they say things like these:

"Fine, go ahead." (Meaning something like "Sure, embarrass me by making a fool of yourself.")

"Please do." (Meaning "You've lost this argument already but I'm going to let you go ahead and pursue this hopelessly stupid path you've chosen so you can apologize to me for the next forty years on this date. A suitable compensation for my patience would be Godiva chocolates, a dozen long-stemmed yellow roses, and, say, oh, maybe three chick flicks without complaint.")

"Please don't" may also fall into this broader category, as when you say, "There's no way I am going to that Tupperware party, even though it is your sister. I'm not going." She says, coldly, perhaps with the added force of The Look.

"Please don't." Gulp. Better go to that Tupperware party, buddy.

"I see." (Meaning "I cannot for the life of me imagine what the hell you are talking about.")

"You don't need to apologize." (Meaning, "If you know what's good for you, apologize. But it won't do any good.")

"Do you think I'm getting fat?" (Meaning, "You better not think I'm getting fat!")

"Whatever you say . . . it's your decision . . . " (Meaning, "Think again, Sparky. It's my way or the highway.")

"Does this outfit look okay?" (Meaning, "Compliment me on this outfit.")

SUGGESTIONS FOR FURTHER PROJECTS

New Woman School items are constantly coming to light as that institution continues to evolve and men slowly but surely are figuring out other Woman School techniques that we've lived with for years but have never fully appreciated. Feel free to write to Man School care of the Publisher with your suggestions and recommendations. If you are a woman and want to complain about your secrets being revealed—well, tough. I'd recommend that you stand up like a woman and face me with your silly kvetching but, well, if things work out the way they're supposed to, by the time this book reaches your hands, I will be living within the Motorbooks International Author Protection Program in the Dominican Republic disguised as a pineapple farmer.

CHAPTER 3

GETTING LUCKY

A woman is a dish for the gods . . . if the devil dress her not.
—SHAKESPEARE, *ANTONY AND CLEOPATRA*

Women think that "getting lucky" is about courtship and love. Well, it isn't. That is a separate chapter altogether, and is, in fact, separated from this one by yet another chapter, "Sex." That's not accidental. Men understand that. Women don't. It's anthropological. Men are looking for a boink, a way to continue their line, to insure the survival of their genes, to move the human race forward. Okay, I think we can be honest here: men are looking for a way to get an hour in the sack with a babe. Or not a babe. Or fifteen minutes. On a picnic table. Or not a picnic table.

Woman is a nest builder. She is looking for a provider, a nurturer for her potential children, a protector from enemy tribes and dinosaurs, a fire starter, a helpmate, a source for a furnished house and a family car she can share with her new boyfriend. A guy says, "Wanna go up to my place, pop a brew, open a can of sardines, and make some crazy monkey love?" The woman hears, "I am ready to make a commitment and cosign on the phone bill."

The woman will be unhappy the next day, in fact, the next six days—because he doesn't call her. When he finds out she is mad at him, he will be amazed. Why would he have called? He hasn't been horny. After all, the moment he *was* horny—about the seventh day—he *did* call. Shouldn't he get some credit for that? No, she says, he shouldn't.

He is using solid male logic. She is using solid female logic. He is speaking Hawaiian. She is speaking Greek. In this cross-gender situation, there is absolutely no exchange of information, no basis for understanding.

But this is the way it is. It's the way it has been for a long time, and frankly, I don't see any signs whatsoever anything is going to change. A wise philosopher (or maybe it was some schlock standup comedian on the Comedy Channel) once said "A man gets married when he thinks this is as good as he's going to do; a woman gets married when she thinks she has something she can work with." I've remembered that wonderful analysis for many, many years. I've remembered that because it is absolutely true, as true as "Righty tighty, lefty loosey." Women are eternal optimists; men get horny every six days. There it is. Bottom line. Point made. Cease fire.

Putting all of these Woman School plans, subterfuges, devices, and weapons in print for you to read is not illegal, immoral, or unethical. All I'm doing here is balancing things in a very small way, hoping to put into the hands of my fellow men some minor means of dealing with the sort of thing women are talking about, discussing, and exchanging on a constant basis. I call to your attention the following paragraph from an issue of the St. Paul, Nebraska, *Phonograph-Herald* newspaper of February 1902.

"A girl may not be able to write poetry nor paint sunsets, but if she can bake a biscuit that is somewhat softer than flint, and can crochet a section of weatherboarding on the gable end of a pair of pantaloons, she may be pretty sure of the approval of some good man."

I rest my case. Some woman was obviously, a century ago, passing along secrets of seduction to other women in her community. What? That was written by a male editor? Never mind.

WHAT EXACTLY ARE WE LOOKING FOR?

This is a book for men, not women, so I am not going to worry about where a woman should look for a good man. In the comic books, I suppose. But let's consider where a man might find a good— or as the case may be—a bad woman. There is another old saying that goes something like "A man wants a saint in the kitchen, a whore in the bedroom." But the thing is, you can get both those things without actually finding a woman with whom you want to use the L word (Love) or, even more seriously, the C word (Commitment).

I know there is a lot of skepticism about it, but I honestly believe in magic when it comes to romance. I believe in love at first sight, I believe in vibes, I believe in romantic chemistry. Although sex, looks, and gymnastic double-jointedness may be a part of that, it certainly isn't the most important part, or even a significant part. There's just something about the right woman, and it is usually an immediate communication. Even if it doesn't happen at first sight, there is a moment when all at once a man thinks, "Holy shit, that is her! It's her! OhmyGod . . .It's her!"

It is not a matter of thought or logic on a man's part. It's not even a matter of being horny. If it is, the relationship is not likely to last very long. I hate to bring tractors back into this book because I promised you this would be about women and relationships and love and other gooey stuff rather than magnetos, carburetors, transmissions, and other gooey stuff, but sometimes I have to fall back on what I understand best because I think that's what you bozos are going to understand best. Ask around why your pals like their cars or sound systems or cigars. Now cut through the baloney about speed, power, style, body, volume, or tone. What do they *really* like about what they like?

You are going to find a veritable swamp of goofy notions about why their preferences are what they are. What their fathers owned, or what the first one they owned happened to be, or about some chick who dug this brand, or where they were the first time they tried this model, and so on. Thing is, they don't have a reason, really. It's romance, pure and simple. Yep, beneath that grease-stained, stinky, unshaven, coarse-languaged oaf is really a mushy, romantical heart.

I don't know what a man wants in a woman, and what's more important, neither does he. We haven't the faintest notion what we want, in fact. Not until the very moment we see it. And then who knows what it is that knocks us goofy?

Does a man really want a supermodel babe? Well, maybe—in his fantasies. But think about it for a moment, as opposed to dreaming about it. Look at yourself in a full-length mirror. Let's say, for the sake of discussion, that somehow, as unlikely as it may seem, you are driving along the highway one day and there is a car alongside the road and it has a flat tire. Someone is sitting behind the wheel (you can't really see even if it is male or female, but you are feeling helpful, maybe even lucky) so you stop to help this person.

It is a woman, and although she is wearing dark glasses, a scarf over her head, and a nondescript light jacket, she has a very soft, nice voice. You tell her to pop the trunk, you drag out the jack and spare, change the tire, tell her through her window that is opened only a crack that the job is done and you hope she has a nice trip. You turn to walk away. She yells through the now opening window, "Can I pay you for your trouble?" You smile and say naw, it's not that big a deal, and you had the time to spare, so . . . She asks if she could at least buy you a drink, the day being so hot and all. She drops her glasses.

Wow. She is really very attractive, maybe even familiar. Beautiful smile. Sure, why not? So you follow her to the next tavern along the way, Ed's Place in Ennui, Nebraska. You help her off with her jacket, she takes the scarf from her gorgeous, flowing hair. And you realize, "My God, It's supermodel Elizabeth Hurley!" She touches your arm, offers to buy you another drink, wonders what you're doing for supper . . .

Well, you know where it's going. You hit it off and she winds up being your main squeeze—Elizabeth Hurley, one of the most beautiful women in the world.

I would like to suggest that at least two things are going to happen here. First, you are no idiot. You know what this incredibly gorgeous creature looks like, and you know what you are. You are going to be worried sick every moment that she is alone that she is going to realize eventually what a ridiculous setup this is and that some hunk (which is to say, any other man, you being the clump you are!) is going to come and take her away.

Secondly, it's not going to be quite as great a situation as you thought. I mean, this is one of the most delicately beautiful women in the world. She is not going to want to mess up that hair, or risk splitting a nail, or get chapped earlobes, let alone do all the other stuff you fantasized about before you ever met her. The first time you make a modest suggestion about what has always seemed like a fun idea to you if you ever wound up in bed with a supermodel, she is going to sputter "You want me to do WHAT with your WHAT?" And you are going to wind up on some sleazy Los Angeles side street paying $36 to a broken-down hooker named Divine Brown, just like Hugh Grant did when he was with Elizabeth Hurley.

So, am I saying what you're really looking for is an ugly girl? No, not at all. In fact, I suggest in my personal consultations with clients at my Love Clinic . . . (Okay, so I don't have a love clinic and even my children don't ask me questions about love and romance, still, this is what I WOULD recommend if I had a Love Clinic and someone asked me, okay?) Where was I? I caution gents about so much as *complimenting* plain girls, even in those panicky minutes following a lonesome evening and immediately following the last call in a town tavern. It's like patting a mangy dog: you're never going to shake that thing.

What I *am* saying is that beauty is a funny thing and rarely what we think it is. Some of the most beautiful women I know have been a surprise to me because I have realized that not everyone else sees that beauty.

This is not true about Linda, I hasten to add. She is out and out beautiful. And that's nice. But far more important to me in the long run is that she is a beautiful soul. For a while there was a gag poster circulating of an incredibly gorgeous woman, half naked, lips parted tantalizingly, eyes half closed, breasts thrust provocatively forward. The text read something like, "No matter what you're thinking, some man somewhere is sick and tired of her s**t." And you *know* that's true.

So, looks are important, but they're not even number five on a list of ten attributes crucial to finding a woman for more than a fling.

FISHING FOR A COMPLEMENT

What we men are looking for, as often as not, is someone who may for all the world seem least likely to be our mate.

One of my favorite people in this world is a big, coarse, loud-mouthed, crude, abrasive, opinionated lout. He was once involved in a modest political campaign with a thoroughly decent young man who was a crusader, but someone who had a cause and wanted to throw his young and Adonis-like body, pure soul and all, onto the fiery pyre of partisan politics.

There was a campaign meeting to consider how to raise money for the brave and noble cause. The cloddish brute in question started off the conversation with the following line: "I move that we rent the Izaak Walton League building and get us a couple Mexican girls and a burro and sell tickets and . . .."

Gasps of utter disbelief stopped the meeting cold. I was there. I know. The Lout looked around in confusion, baffled by the horrified looks of everyone in the room. The stunned candidate said, "My God, man—the ethics . . . " And the big klutz responded, "Well, sure, but ethics aside . . . "

This would be a good place to take a break. Put down this book, go get a sandwich, watch an episode of *COPS*, twist a rusty bolt off of the tractor you're restoring, and consider the depravity of the man I am introducing you to. Consider that he is fat, not particularly handsome except in a Jabba the Hut sort of way, sweats a lot, smokes bad tobacco, and spits when he talks. He is also magnificently successful in his profession, and I adore this man, so I am not at all insulting him. In fact, in many ways, the above description might be of me.

Brace yourself. This guy married a nun. Yep, and not one of those Nunzillas who hit your knuckles with a ruler and brought down the wrath of God on your soul because you didn't clap the erasers quite right after school. No, this guy married a slight, slim, pretty, quiet, delicate, modest, sensitive, artistic, submissive, gentle, gentle nun. And they have been married a long time. With a single word she can tame him, reduce him to a love-slave, make him sit quietly in a corner reciting his alphabet. She hasn't civilized him. He's still the guy she married, as all men are still the men all women have married, but she can, for a moment, reduce him to a manageable pile of rubble.

A CAUTION

One of the things you'll really want to keep in mind as you study and consider the various alternative methodologies for finding, approaching, and winning a woman is that while you, through this book, are for the first time in human history being educated, in a rudimentary way, in matters that women have known for millenniums through Woman School, you are in a struggle against very heavy odds. Women go into the battle of the sexes armed with thermonuclear weapons delivered on laser-guided smart missiles; meanwhile, you are standing there for all the world as nekkid as a jaybird, holding a sharp stick.

There will certainly come a time when you are going to say to yourself, "Self, that Welsch guy must be an idiot. Or maybe this woman sitting across the table from me is one in a billion. Because she isn't even remotely like the women he describes in that book of his. She agrees with everything I'm saying. She thinks it's cute when I stick string beans up my nose and bark like a walrus. She doesn't mind at all that she's wearing a nice new dress and I'm wearing jeans and a sweatshirt. She says she really enjoyed seeing *Robocop XII* and thinks it will be fine if we spend next weekend watching professional football on television and have nothing to eat but potato chips, garlic dip, and beer."

Don't fool yourself for a minute, kid. It's a setup. Don't believe those lips. Try not to be taken in by those eyes. And as for the boobs, well, you are for all the world seeing the same thing the mouse sees just before he digs into that cheese buffet set up for him on the little piece of wood and wire someone kindly left for him behind the refrigerator.

I don't expect you to listen to me. I don't imagine for a moment that anything I am saying will make one bit of difference to you. But just remember that you heard it here first. And try to teach your sons well. Okay, of course they won't listen either, but still . . .

Most men are existentialists along the line of black Lab retrievers: they are simply there. There is no introspection, no self-evaluation, no personality inventory, no careful examination in a magnifying mirror to determine if those eyebrows should arch just a touch more. I have never seen one of my buddies searching his hair for split ends. In fact, I'm betting I could get into a fight suggesting he should. If I should mention that he has split ends, the odds are about a thousand to one he's either going to tell me where I can put my split ends or he'll recap the last play in the football game we're watching.

But if you are going woman shopping, you might want to give this question some thought; while it might not make any particular difference to who you are, after all, it sure is going to be something that crosses her mind, and probably early on in the negotiations.

Who Exactly Are You?

Elsewhere in these pages I will discuss the proper procedure for male behavior while *living* with a female but at this point I am talking about courtship, and courtship sure isn't the same situation as it will be once the deal is nailed down. We all know that. During this stage of a relationship, the woman in question is applying an especially rigorous set of tests to decide if she is going to grace the man in question with her, um, favors. So it's incumbent on the male in the contest to put forth just a trifle more effort in feigning civilization than he intends to once the deal is struck. Once her clothes are hung in the closet, then you can go ahead and act like the pig you are. I think we all pretty much understand that, right?

We all know you are going to fart. Eventually everyone does. It is a natural process and most males consider flatulence to be one of the most entertaining processes of the human body. Or, for that matter, the nonhuman body, I guess. Every man I know thoroughly enjoys a dog well accomplished in farting. If you don't believe me, get yourself a farting dog, encourage him with a hearty meal of corn fritters or savory baked beans, and invite some of your buddies over to watch a football game.

Watch your buddies' reactions as the dog indulges himself in a vigorous volley of SBDs. While we're on the subject, why are all dog farts SBDs? Is it the lack of cheeks? Is it a survival characteristic left over from their days in the jungles? Or do they simply believe in the widely held theory that there is more than a casual link between the S and the D? Is one of the reasons an SBD is so D is that it is so S, energy otherwise expended in vocalizations, so to speak, dissipates the olfactory assault, or conversely, the conservation of auditory energies amplifying instead the phenomenon's redolence? Excuse the heavy-duty scientific-philosophical discussion here but this is obviously a question to which I have given some thought.

Anyway, where was I? Oh, yeah. Prime your pooch for a particularly spectacular fartfest and watch your buddies' reactions. They will laugh hilariously. They will forget the football, no matter how exciting it is, and roll on the floor in glee. Sure, they will fan the air, hold their noses, spray household fresheners, and curse the dog. But I guarantee you that they will: 1) laugh themselves sick, and 2) talk about the evening with nothing but joy and pleasure in the telling for the rest of their lives.

This social experiment is even better if you can find one of those rare dogs who reacts to his own farts. There is simply nothing funnier than a dog who farts, jumps to his feet, stares at the imaginary spot where the offending orifice was at the time of the infraction, and stomps off huffily, as if YOU were the one who committed the crime. I once had a dog like this. You cannot imagine the hours of entertainment that dog provided. I once met a dog that would bark at his butt when he farted. That's even funnier.

This is not the kind of entertainment I would recommend for a first date, or even a second date, or even for a fifth wedding anniversary. Little girls think farts are hilarious, mostly because they are, of course. In fact, nothing is funnier than little girls farting, not even dogs farting, mostly because little girls still have the pre—Woman School innocence and wonder that gives them permission to enjoy a good fart just like a man enjoys a good fart.

First there is the feminine, juvenile tweet, almost a parody of *real* farting, but even that thoroughly funny method is enhanced by the unrestrained and infectious giggling that is certain to erupt any time one of two or more girls fart. It is truly an exercise in utterly innocent, completely genuine human hilarity.

But in Woman School, apparently, young women are taught to restrain their glee. My guess is so they'll have increased leverage over the men in their lives, being able to assume a haughty and superior air about such crude behavior.

That is to say, women think farts are funny too. I mean, jeez, how could they NOT think farts are funny? But by feigning indignation or even disgust, they can make the man in the room look like a pig. And that's what it's all about, right? What I wonder is, do women just go ahead and have flatulent fun when men aren't around? Do women relax and fire away, say, at a quilting bee or baby shower? Do they discuss how funny a fart is, and how much funnier it is that they have intimidated men into straining and spraining their guts to observe the totally goofy household rules about farting that women have set up in mockery of nature? I don't know.

Maybe before I write the next volume of this encyclopedia some woman, haunted by the hypocritical double standard will step forward and say, "Rog, wait until you hear this. I was at a meeting of the Baptist church women last year and after a dinner of baked beans, cole slaw, and Aunt Emily's sausage casserole, well, we were moving some chairs around the room when . . . ." Then, gentlemen, we will know.

One might discuss the ground rules for one's own ventings in detail with the woman of your heart's desire about the same time you determine you are going to formalize your relationship and are working at figuring out what you're going to do about family finances.

I'm not just talking marriage here. I think this farting issue is important enough that it should be aired, as it were, early on in a relationship. At will? In the front room? During a particularly funny Jay Leno monologue? In the bedroom? In the car? If she should insist that such behavior will never be tolerated under any circumstances anywhere—and some women will demand such a totally impossible physiological restraint—rent an educational video about people who have spontaneously combusted. Tell her it's no mystery at all why now and then people explode in spontaneous fiery methane fireballs; in your role as a secret agent before you met her, you saw the classified government files attributing such human fireballs to excessive methane retention. She may not buy it, but what do you have to lose?

GIRDING LOINS

If you are at that stage in your life when you are looking for babes, it is really important to maintain your very best physical conditioning because a woman, anthropologists tell us, is looking for a suitable father for her children. On the other hand, as you probably also know if you are at this stage in your life, you don't want to look *too* physically fit or you're going to spend most of your time fending off advances from gay guys. (I assume that since you are reading this primer about looking for babes, such advances would not be welcome.)

Once you're married, it is really important that you let down, get fat and slovenly, relax, get in some quality couch time because otherwise your woman is going to figure you're fooling around. She figures that since you have now landed the most perfect woman in the world, what possible reason could you have to keep up your competitive edge? You owe it to her to demonstrate your reliability by going soft.

When courting, bathe and shave with tedious regularity. Dress fancy. Don't even let on that you *own* overalls, much less wear them. During your courting years, just tuck away all those wonderfully comfortable, roomy, beloved tatters you treasure most. Try to listen to what *she* says about your choice in sartorial splendor.

Because the male auditory system is not at all the same as the female's, a woman may say something you may not hear or immediately detect the importance of. For example, when she asks you, "Are you going to wear those shoes to the party?" she is not *really* asking you if those are the shoes you going to wear to the party. Believe me, that's not what she's saying.

I hope you have read the chapter on male/female language disparity carefully. It applies in almost every other chapter of this book. What a woman says is not what a man hears; what a man says is not what a woman hears. Same words, different language. In German there are words like "Gift," "Artiste," "Eis," and "Fahrt." They mean, respectively, "poison" (imagine the potential consequences of THAT confusion!), "stripper," "ice cream" ("bourbon and ice" in German is not a tidy drink), and "voyage."

Same thing in English with "dressing up." When Linda gets up in the morning, she puts on makeup, even if the big plans for the day are feeding the dogs twice. She doesn't like to have anyone, including the dogs, see her hair in rollers. For me, dressing for the day includes getting up. If we are going to town for supper, I like to check to see if my fly is closed. If it's a formal deal, I might put on clean overalls. For an audience with the Pope or dinner at the White House, I put on underwear.

My buddies Woodrow and Lunchbox have demonstrated particular skill, I think, in dealing with our society's sartorial demands on ordinary men. They dress in work clothes and overalls pretty much all the time. I don't recall ever seeing them both in a suit and tie. Although I *have* seen *each* of them in a suit and tie. In fact, in *the* suit and tie. See, thing is, being practical, they know there are times in life when you need to wear a suit and tie, like at funerals. So they have a suit. One suit. And they just hope no one they both know dies. It works very well for them and I can't help but think that it helps someone like me stay alive, simply knowing the inconvenience it would cause those two to have to decide who would attend my funeral and who would have to watch from the trees outside the cemetery fence. In his overalls.

DRESSING FOR SUCCESS

You'll have to work around this kind of inclination for courtship. You are going to have to look like you love tight collars, silly neckties, binding pants, uncomfortable shoes, and scraping hair off your face. Women expect it. And then you can just ease into normal living sometime after the wedding. Like later on the next morning. She'll understand. She's seen her father.

But for now, put away the comfortable clothes. You can take them out now and again and remember what it was like to be comfortable, maybe even put them on in the privacy of your own home. But if you intend to get a woman who is something beyond what you *deserve* (and believe me, you don't want the kind of woman you *deserve!*) you are going to have to maintain this false image as long and thoroughly as you can for a while. Again, as with your physical conditioning, you not only *can* let down once you've solidified your gains, you *should*. This will clearly show that you are done shopping and are perfectly happy at home with the most perfect woman of all.

And for Pete's sake, park the battered blue 1984 Ford F-150 pickup truck with the body so rusted out you can watch the pavement pass beneath your feet as you drive. If you have to, rent a car. I cannot for the life of me imagine why a woman (or anyone else, for that matter) is impressed by a man's car. (The most rotten schmucks on the face of the earth have fancy, expensive cars.) But they are. So get a fancy, expensive car.

You're also going to have to figure out some way to look like you have a lot of money. It's okay to be cheap with everyone else, even when you are with her, but you want to make it darn clear that when it comes to her, money means nothing. On the other hand, you are also going to want to leave the clear impression that you have a job and are *earning* that money. If you spend like an African dictator but don't have a job, it is going to occur to her sooner or later, if she sticks around, she will be the earner in the family, and you will be the spender. Not good. (By the way, women always have jobs. I don't know why that is. If I had to guess, I'd say Woman School!)

ELITE FEAT

Remember, gents: women are not like you. They are not looking for a couple hours of fun drinking beer, dancing, and playing pool, then a quick roll in the hay, a good night's sleep, friendly fare-thee-well, and fond memories. They see this dating and courtship process as preparation for a lifetime. To a woman, a date with you is an audition, a screen test, a matter of comparative shopping. Most men don't even know they have a lifetime. Men certainly don't see one evening's $20 investment as a cue for the lady at the organ to begin pounding away at "The Wedding March."

One of the things a woman is going to want to look at is your social standing, and I don't mean the circle of your best buddies. In fact, I really *don't* mean your best buddies. Anything *but* your best buddies. When you are going out with her, especially on early dates, especially if you are thinking there might be later dates, stay out of that tavern where you have spent weekends and off-work hours for the last ten years. You don't want her to see that, take it from me. God only knows what other women might have written about you on the walls in the ladies room in that tavern, after all.

And nothing squelches a possible closer moment, if you catch my drift, than a barmaid smiling, pinching your butt, and asking, "What are you drinking, Big Rog? Your usual? Or what you usually order when you're trying to get some dumb chick into the sack?" I don't care how masculine you are, you can probably see a problem developing here.

Until you have things rolling along pretty well, your best bet is to pretend that you simply don't have any friends, or that they're far away, maybe involved in the making of a movie in the south of France, or doing secret missions with the CIA, or on a mercy mission to care for poor children in Venezuela.

You definitely want to keep her away from your family. Chances are, your family will like her. And be ready to talk about all the cute things you did as a boy, and all the dumb things you did as a teenager, and all the hideously stupid moves you've made as an adult. Or how great your first wife was, and how you never appreciated her, and how your fooling around and drinking ruined that marriage, and . . . well, you get the idea.

Worse, she may take a liking to your brother.

THE MARITAL ARTS

It's up to you whether you tell a woman if you've been married before. That may be something you'll want to save until later. But you may want to think fairly seriously about telling her if you *are* currently married. (Engagement is another thing altogether. Some women see that condition as a challenge while most women think of marriage as an institution as sacred as the death sentence.)

If you are married, and you don't tell her, and there is any chance at all of her finding out later, or your wife finding out later, it is really important that you check on the status of your life insurance policies and talk to an agent soon about some high-figure term life. It will seem expensive but since you're only going to need it for a month or so, it'll wind up being fairly cheap. You can just thank your lucky stars you're not going to be around when everyone finds out who the beneficiary is.

NOT FOR A COON'S AGE

The smartest people in the world were the Pawnee Indians. If we had paid more attention to what they had to say rather than spending all that energy stealing their land, we would be one heck of a lot better off. The Pawnee marriage system was a loose sort of arrangement, mostly of convenience and inclination. Did they love each other? You bet they did, but they weren't dumb enough to think for a moment that such feelings don't change over time nor that there are many factors in determining love and marriage stability aside from gooey love. If you were a Pawnee, you were pretty much married when you both said you were, and pretty much unmarried when one of you said you were. Makes sense.

Here's the good part: unions were mostly between older men and younger women, older women and younger men. The theory was, an old man knows exactly what a fine thing a young woman is and treats her the way a young woman wants to be treated. Moreover, an old man knows the value of taking his time in the buffalo robes, doesn't make a lot of demands, is just thankful to the point of breaking down and crying when he snuggles down for the night beside a luscious eighteen-year-old beauty who can't believe that he actually has the stamina to want to do it once again. ("That's twice this month alone! What a man you are!")

A young girl likes the attention of an old man. A young coed sleeping with a grizzled old faculty member once explained that situation to me very articulately: "I love sleeping with Old Bert: he's always so grateful!"

An older woman knows how to please a man and like her male elder counterpart knows how to enjoy the energy—and probably even the efficiency—of a young man. He's ready to go often but doesn't waste a lot of her time or keep her up all hours raising carnal hell. And a young man doesn't really care what he's getting as long as he's getting.

It sure is a good thing our Christian pioneer forefathers charged right in and screwed up . . . uh, straightened out those heathen Pawnee savages, right?

AN APPRECIATION FOR YOUNGER WOMEN

When Linda and I were first dating she came roaring up to my house one weekend, tears running down her face, and sputtered that her fiancé, with whom she was breaking up in anticipation of hooking up with this old guy, had told her during one of those end-of-relationship arguments that some friends of his in my area of the state had gossiped that " . . . That Roger Welsch reputedly has a taste for younger women!" She was really troubled by this charge.

I looked up from whatever I was doing, pretty much flummoxed, and said, "Well, I do have a taste for younger women. Like you!" Linda paused just long enough to do some quick arithmetic, figured out that, she is indeed eighteen years younger than me, and drove off, presumably to tell her fading flame that, yes, Rog DOES have a taste for younger women, and God bless him for it!

Just as American and Pawnee twenty-year-old men are alike, it turns out that forty-five-year-old white guys are pretty much like forty-five-year-old Indian guys too. Now, admittedly, there is a certain amount of a trophy-bride attitude here (snow on the roof, but fire in the furnace!), but any old goat like me who is tinkering with the idea of taking on a young woman needs to be prepared for a certain amount of comment, not always in a spirit of admiration for his virility.

Linda and I had been married only a short time when I was talking with Butch Williams, legendary house mover, about hauling a home onto this farmland for us. He looked over Linda and me a moment and then drawled, "You two remind me of the old gent who married the young girl and told her, 'If I'm ever out in the fields and you feel like some lovin', just step out on the porch and fire the shotgun and I'll come runnin'.' The poor old guy died two weeks into pheasant season."

Actually, that's a pretty gentle one. They can get rougher: Old guy marries the younger woman, and one night while playing around in bed, he pats on her the breasts and says, "You know, if those gave milk, we could get rid of the cow!" And he laughed at his own joke, while the bride muttered to herself. A moment or so later, he patted her on her naughty bit and laughed, "You know, if that thing would lay eggs, we could get rid of the chickens!" Again she muttered. "What are you mumbling about?" the old man finally asked, whereupon she patted him on his Mr. Happy and said, "If that thing would get up and go to work, we could get rid of the hired man."

> *That's the nature of women . . . not to love when we love them, and to love when we love them not.*
> —CERVANTES, *DON QUIXOTE*

There are, of course, also stories that reflect an opposite reality: An old guy was getting a physical examination in anticipation of marrying a woman half his age. He mentioned to the doctor that he hoped he and his new bride would soon have children on the way, but the doctor laughed that if he expected to have children, he really should consider taking on a hired hand at the farm. The next time the doctor saw him, he asked about the family situation and the old farmer grinned that yep, the wife was indeed pregnant. "So, you took my advice about taking on a hired hand then, huh?" the doctor asked. "Yeppers," the old man said, "And she's pregnant too!"

Probably the most devastating comment I have ever gotten about being married to a woman eighteen years younger than I am came from my own father, who always seemed to have a perfect story ready for any situation. Linda and I had been married a short time and were having supper with my parents at their home. After dessert, I said, "Mom, Dad, I have an announcement to make." Mom put her head down on the table and my old German father sat there stolidly, knowing that my announcements are rarely reason to rejoice.

I knew this was going to be somewhat unsettling news I was about to report. It had been bad enough that I had gotten the first divorce ever known in the countless millenniums of my family's history, and that I had married a Catholic, a Czech, a woman two decades younger than me. And don't get me wrong: the folks love Linda. In fact, they've said that if we break up they want to keep her and get rid of me, but still, it wasn't easy for them to deal with in the beginning.

Now I was about to tell them that we were going to have a baby, in September, the same time my daughter Jen was going to have a baby. (As it turned out, Jen had her baby on Wednesday, we had Antonia on Friday, so my granddaughter is slightly older than our daughter!) And I knew it wouldn't be seemly in their eyes for me, an old goat, to start a second family with this young woman.

My announcement met stunned silence. After a minute or so, Dad said, "Rog, let me tell you a story. There once was an old man out hunting in the woods one day, and he saw a bear. He raised his cane and yelled as loud as he could, 'Bang!' There was a young man in the woods at the same time and he aimed and shot at that same bear at the very moment the old man yelled 'Bang!' Rog, that bear fell dead, and to this day, the old man thinks he killed that bear with his cane."

At that moment, I loved my old man more, I think, than ever before or ever after. It was as if he had saved that perfect story for just this perfect moment, as if he had spent all his life waiting for his only son to marry a woman eighteen years his junior and announce some day that they were going to have a child.

If you ever court a woman more than ten years younger than you, you might just as well resign yourself to years of stories like that.

All Hail the Harmless Elders

I spend a lot of time in Native American culture and so I'm a little spoiled by their profound respect for age. They have this peculiar notion that a guy sixty-five years old might actually have learned something in fifty years that a fifteen-year-old hasn't. That doesn't seem to be the case in modern America, where fifteen-year-olds somehow manage to circulate freely within society, absolutely confident that they are unappreciated geniuses, when the fact of the matter is, someone should slap them around until they're cross-eyed.

I would like to suggest that anyone over sixty-five should have some special recognition beyond a pathetic social security check, inadequate health insurance, free fishing permits, and a dime off Big Macs. I think that men who are sixty-five years old or older should be issued a Harmless Old Geezer card. This permit would allow old farts to make suggestive comments to women, pat them on the ass, play footsie uninvited, stare at women and make disgusting noises of appreciation, touch dancers in strip joints where touching is not allowed, ask suggestive questions of women anytime anywhere and drool. They'd be seated next to the best-looking women in the house at all occasions and receive free passes to topless bars and strip joints, free naughty girl calendars, complimentary subscriptions to skin magazines, and passes to nude beaches. They would also have permission to yell at women—on the streets, in theaters or restaurants, and permission to throw small stones at passing automobiles, that kind of thing.

Everyone is always trying to take things away from us elderly—driving privileges, for example. Give me the things I've listed in the paragraph above and I'd gladly do my part to increase highway safety by surrendering my driver's license right here and now. The logic is impeccable: I should be off the highway because I pose a special hazard and therefore impose on the larger society all kinds of expenses and problems. I'm no threat to women. Anything I might propose is laughable.

My Harmless Old Geezer card would simply make that condition explicit: "Humor this old guy. Sure, he's annoying, maybe even disgusting, but he is generally harmless. Let him pat your girlfriend or wife on the ass. What harm can it do? Make his golden years a little easier. Don't forget, your time is coming."

Linda has pointed out that this kind of license could possibly lead some men into excessive and obnoxious behavior. Okay, okay, she said it could possibly lead *me* into excessive and obnoxious behavior. She therefore recommends that the card have a little margin of punch numbers around it, thus limiting the geezer in question to, say, fifty-two exercises in obnoxious behavior per year. That strikes me as being excessively restrictive. I would like to see maybe 365 punches, but I'm not sure how that would work.

Maybe something like those debit-credit cards. I think this could come to change offensive behavior to something not simply acceptable but even affirmative. I can imagine women talking with each other and saying things like, "Yep, that old guy really is a cute little rascal. And to think that he gave up his only credit for obnoxious behavior left for the week just to pinch my ass! I consider it quite a compliment, actually. In fact, my bottom has collected sixteen Old Geezer credits already this week. I think I'm just getting more attractive every month if you go by the credits I'm burning up for these old farts!"

I firmly believe that my Harmless Old Geezer card could change how we look at our golden years and how women feel about what is laughingly called sexual harassment, and how they decide where to sit on a bus.

What about older women and younger men? I don't know anything about what goes on with older women and younger men. Maybe that's covered in Woman School. It's none of my business. It's been a long time since I've been a younger man.

CHAPTER 4

FINDING
A BABE

Of all of the paths that lead to a woman's love,
Pity's the straightest.

—JOHN FLETCHER, *THE KNIGHT OF MALTA*

Now, this is really getting complicated, I know. What are we looking for a babe FOR? Are we thinking "bride for a night?" Well, in that case, all we really need to do is down a couple shots of Wild Turkey or Southern Comfort and the problem is solved: any woman who is not disgusted enough to throw her drink in your face and walk away is, at this point, a babe.

But if we are thinking something a good deal more serious, you know, having your children, building a future, going fishing, trusting with your best friend, admitting human frailty, eating her cooking, or leaving the toilet seat up, then we need to take a totally different tack. And we need to remember for whom we are scouting for a woman. That is to say, you. Or me. And what is going to work for you is almost certainly not going to work for me.

I have given this problem a lot of thought. I tend to be fairly certain about a lot of things, but this one still has been scratching my bean. Where to find the perfect babe? For you? Whew . . . . tough question!

We can start with the story I told you about my friend and his wife, however, you know, the one where the loud, obnoxious slob married the gentle, quiet, sweet nun. This has to be one of the most underrated, ignored situations in our society: probably no phrase is used more in America today than "How did *she* wind up with *him*?" I know a lot of people have asked that about Linda and me. In fact, Linda's folks have asked that about Linda and me. In fact, Linda has asked that about Linda and me.

We are total opposites. We have only a couple things in common but Linda won't let me tell you about them, because she's too shy to share that kind of intimate detail. This makes my point, because I'd be perfectly tickled to tell you the details and even draw some diagrams.

One thing I can tell you: we both have a sense of humor, but even there we are quite different. Linda is a wit. Out of absolutely nowhere she comes up with stunning lines, perfectly phrased, perfectly timed. I almost wet myself two or three times a day at her stunning gag lines. I have a good ear, on the other hand: I know a good line when I hear it and I have absolutely no reluctance in stealing it. This makes us, in our oppositeness, a pretty good match.

It's the yin-yang thing: you are not two of the same element, you are two separate parts of a whole. You know how sickologists [sic] suggest to cloddish males that they get in touch with their feminine side? I think that's what relationships are all about. Getting in touch with the less obvious parts of yourself, but through another person, which is a lot more fun, especially when it comes to the sex thingies.

PLENTY OF PLACES NOT TO LOOK

But the point is, if you are a Ping-Pong nut for example—you just can't pass up a good international Ping-Pong tourney—I would use some caution in assuming that you should start cruising the crowds at Ping-Pong conventions looking for babes. Do you see the problem? There's a good chance that once the charm of your backspin wears off, she is sooner or later going to have to say something like, "Do you know that every time you crouch down to receive a serve, you show about six inches of butt crack? It drives me nuts. It's really disgusting." On the other hand, if you hook up with a Minneapolis-Moline tractor nut, she's never going to notice your butt crack serve reception because she is going to be at a tractor show across town when you're playing Ping-Pong at the Y.

It would bother some men that their women are not at all interested in their consuming passion, but believe me, their interest can be pretty suffocating. Besides, I'm betting that your Minneapolis-Moline tractor babe is also going to notice your obnoxious nether-décolletage soon enough herself, and make an issue of it, and make you start wearing hip-wader underwear. Women just do that.

There are a lot of places where you might look for a woman who would be compatible with your notion of fun: a fishing show, a topless bar, a police lineup. But she may be there because she already has a man in her life, and she is at this location only because her stud muffin is there and she's trying to understand his particular way of thinking. In cases like this, you are not only running up against a woman who is already wrestling with someone as dense and difficult as you, but if you start making your moves on this woman too soon, you are likely also to run up against the dense and difficult one himself, who may not only be as dense and difficult as you, but also a lot bigger and meaner. Maybe even armed.

NAKED TRUTH

How about a strip joint? Now, that would seem like a perfect context for mate shopping. Looking over strippers you should be able to get a darn good idea of exactly what the package is, right? What kind of sense does it make to make life choices when you have no idea what's underneath all those clothes? So, hey, maybe a good place to start this babe shopping process is with naked babes, right?

Well, it may not be as easy as it seems. I once was teaching a seminar at a university, maybe ten students. One day I accidentally picked up a *Playboy* magazine in a local grocery store thinking it was a gardening periodical I was looking for and before I realized what had happened, I accidentally had gone through the *Playboy* Advisor, all the cartoons, and a pictorial on the girls of the (then) Big Eight. There was a large photo of one of the young ladies in my class, in her altogether. She was looking over her shoulder, smiling coyly, apparently mistaking the reader for her proctologist.

The next day in class I noticed that this coed was actually a good deal more attractive than I had noticed up to this point. She had been a very nice-looking young lady, but somehow she now took on something more of an air of true and solid babedom. Maybe I hadn't noticed her natural beauty because in class she wore glasses— and clothes. I noticed too that after class, she was met immediately at the classroom door by a huge football player who surrounded her as she moved trippingly down the hallway. This told me two things, me being an intellectual sort of guy and all: first, when you have a woman like that, you damn well better be a football player; and if you have any intentions of putting the moves on a woman like this, you better be prepared to have the living bejesus kicked out of you. Unless you are a football player.

All in all, I think *Playboy* models may not be the best choice for a relationship unless you like street brawls and you have a really good health-insurance program. That goes double for strippers, who are generally more immediately accessible and therefore a darn sight more dangerous. A friend of mine once said that he considers the *National Geographic* magazine and *Playboy* to be pretty much the same, both showing exotic and beautiful places we'll never get to visit.

MORE RESEARCH

Just as I am something of an expert when it comes to dating, I have also spent some time studying the sociology of the strip joint— although I got something of a slow start. I was, in fact, sixty years old and out for a night's revelry in the big city (Lincoln, Nebraska) with an old friend, John Carter, and a new friend, Jim Harrison, a writer. We were returning from a great supper and our cab was circling the hotel for a curbside landing when Jim pointed to a brightly lit establishment behind the hotel, garishly signaling itself to be The Night Before.

"What's that? A strip joint?" Jim asked.

"I don't know," I returned snappily, figuring that an accomplished intellectual like Jim would expect a witty dialogue. Then I made a big mistake. I added, "I've never been to a strip joint."

The cabbie slid the vehicle to a stop and turned in his seat to join Jim and John in staring at me in wonder. "How old are you?" the cabbie asked. "And you've never been to a strip joint?"

Before I could utter "nope," John and Harrison dragged me from the cab and into The Night Before. It was an instructive exercise. For one thing, I had, for some reason, always had the notion that women who take off their clothes and dance on bar tops, swinging from trapezes like lemurs, would probably pretty much look like lemurs. Nope. These women were as gorgeous as I'd ever seen in my life, and they were nekkid as jaybirds and about as friendly as you can imagine, although they seemed considerably friendlier to Jim, as ugly as he is, than they were to me, as rosy cheeked and wholesome as I am. It may have had something to do with the fact that he was strewing $5 bills around the place like rice at a wedding while I was trying to figure out where to put my quarters. (You'd be surprised if I told you where the young ladies dancing on the bar told me I could put my quarters. Or maybe you wouldn't.)

Aside from the immense pleasure I found in watching the wonders of God's creation pass in front of my appreciative eyes, I also got two of the funniest lines I've ever heard in my life. Someone came in and noticed John Carter drooling on the edge of the dancer's platform and sputtered, "John Carter? Aren't you the John Carter who's a curator at the State Historical Society?"

John, with more aplomb than he should ever have mustered considering the fact that a gorgeous pair of breasts were at that very moment dancing marvelously about three inches from the end of his nose, responded, "I come here for the music!"

The other great line came the next day when I reported honestly and gleefully to Linda where I'd been the night before and what I'd seen. She listened impassively, and then noted a lipstick stain on my shirt collar. She said, "That better be the color John Carter wears."

I talked my way out of any further domestic problems by explaining that my two pals had lied to me, telling me that The Night Before is actually the Nebraska Center for Interpretive Dance and only after we were back at the hotel did they reveal to me that I had actually been in a strip joint. Yeah, I know. Linda didn't buy that story either.

FURTHER BABE-ING VENUES

Never bring romance into the workplace. For one thing, after inventorying all day in the rubber band factory, do you really want to drive home with the woman you've been working beside all day, talk more rubber bands, then talk rubber bands over martinis, and then over lasagna, and then comment on the inappropriate use of rubber bands on *Ally McBeal*, and then enjoy some rubber-band pillow talk?

The office is where you flirt and fool around, not where you court. If you make your workplace a serious courting arena, then when you settle down, your new mate is going to realize that you use your workplace as a courting arena. She will henceforth see to it that she has a major role in the hiring, assignments, firing, and organizing Christmas parties at your workplace for the rest of your miserable life.

I used to work in a university English department. There were lots of really ugly and unreasonable rules against putting the moves on coeds. I can understand that. It simply wouldn't be fair to expect a poor innocent twenty-year-old woman to deal maturely with a smooth-talking, suave, worldly, slick son of a gun like me. And if you believe something that stupid, you've never met a coed or an English department faculty member. But those are the rules.

There are other babes besides coeds in higher education. At this moment I am sitting here dreamily staring off through my office window, remembering Linda and LeAnn, the secretarial hotties of that English department. I remember how they used to chase me into the mailroom and slam and lock the door. I would make gestures feigning an effort to protect my virtue, my dignity, but there were, after all two of them, and if I resisted too much, all of my Xerox stuff would come back to me all crumpled up the next day and miscollated. Or I would arrive at school one day, after word got out I was seeing someone else, to find every surface in my office (door knobs, typewriter keys, and drawer pulls) coated with Vaseline.

If you are going to look for babes at the college level, take my advice and look at the secretaries. Besides, they have jobs and are earning a living. Do I listen to my own advice? My Lovely Linda was a secretary. At the university. Okay, *sometimes* it's okay to fool around in the workplace, but only if it seems appropriate. Or fun. Or like something you're going to be able to get away with.

CHECKING OUT THE LAY OF THE LAND

I would think that county fairs would be a good place to look for a babe. If you find out nothing else about her, you will know that she makes a fair-to-middlin' plum jelly, sews a blue-ribbon quilt, and can play the domination game with yearling calves—a real asset when it comes to raising children or husbands.

Some friends have suggested to me that an estate auction might be a good place to look for a babe. You can tell from how the sale is going what kind of money the widow is going to have. My friends figure that if she is auctioning off, say, a whole shop full of wood-working tools, then she has been accustomed to dealing with a guy who collects tools and works in the shop every evening and weekend.

But how can you be sure she's not selling off all this stuff because she is sick and tired of a guy who smells like wood dust and casein glue? In fact, how can you be sure she didn't poison him specifically because she wanted to get all these chisels, lathes, and clamps out of her life? You might want to strike up a conversation with the grieving widow before you make your move.

Perhaps you're the shy type and aren't ready to pop questions like, "I guess your husband was quite a guy when it came to inserting a tenon into a mortise, then, huh?" There are other ways to get information about what pleases or displeases a woman. Divorce court comes to mind. Just go hang around the courthouse on days when divorces are being settled before the judge and you'll find out what sort of financial situation the object of your potential affections will have, what she likes and for-damn-certain what she doesn't like, how big and ugly her former husband is, the extent of his gun collection, his record of previous assaults, all of which is information that can be useful in courtship.

PARKING PLACES

There's been a lot said about going to parks for woman shopping. Some writers even suggest taking along a small, borrowed child by way of bait, in effect trolling for babes. This almost certainly works, but if you use this device, you are juggling with hand grenades. The old line about a ticking biological clock may be a cliché, but fellas, it's a true one. Nothing is more dangerous than a woman who thinks her chances for having children are slipping away with discarded calendar pages. If you like and want children, well, that's fine. But if you don't, your feelings aren't going to make much difference if you take up with this ovarial factory coyly running her fingers up and down your arm and nibbling your fingers. Inside her somewhere there are hundreds of little baby-eggs screaming "Yes, mommy, go get him! Make him do it! Set us free!"

And she will.

Once a woman has children, she has no greater drive than to protect them, to make sure they are well sheltered, fed, and educated. You are sitting there in that lounge sucking on the ice cubes from your Jack Daniels and she is sipping at the remnants of a daiquiri. You ask if she'd like another; she says sure. And you begin to have visions of a wonderful night in her bed.

That's not what she sees. She sees private school tuition payments, separate bedrooms for each of her four kids at home, military school for the boy who just burned down the neighbor's garage, therapy for the girl with bulimia, unlimited orthodontics all around, a final settlement for all her nasty educational loans, an apartment for her invalid mom, treatments for her old man's drinking problem, and a replacement for that aging car whose squealing, failing hydraulics wake up the entire neighborhood every time she turns the corner too tight coming out of the garage.

From my experience, there's a very good chance that both parties will get what they want, but the man will never know what hit him.

HEALTH CAN BE DANGEROUS
TO YOUR HEALTH

A gym offers a chance to see a woman sweating in skimpy clothing, but for me this is way too much like cruising for babes in health food stores. There is some very real danger that a woman who believes in keeping in shape is going to think you should do the same thing. Moreover, why is she working so hard to get into shape? Because if she doesn't work out every day, in two weeks she turns into the Goodyear blimp? We don't want that, now, do we? Or is she so desperate to get a man she'll do anything, including working out like a sweat hog to get one? If that's the case, what's the problem that has thrown her into this last, desperate gesture of self-improvement? You may not want to know.

PLAYING NURSIE

I always thought a nurse would make a great wife. She can tend to your injuries and all, but mostly because she studied anatomy and so she knows things. Just things. I thought that if I ever found myself in a situation where I was back into the market, I could save myself a lot of time and trouble by concentrating on nurses, because with my sense of grace and coordination, I spend more time in emergency wards with nurses than in fancy lounges with airline stewardesses.

But the more I look at this situation, the less sure I am of its wisdom. Over the past few years I have spent some time in medical situations and I have found that nurses are not easily impressed, even by a rugged, good-looking guy like me. For example, a couple years ago I had an operation for a heart problem. The doctor gave me my preliminary exam and instructions for the procedure. As I was checking out of his office, I stopped by the nurses' station to get some further printed material and I commented that I was really confused because he had told me that I shouldn't be lifting anything over twenty pounds for at least two weeks after the operation and, as I commented to the four or five nurses standing at the station, I wondered then how I was supposed to pee.

What I hadn't considered was that the next morning, I'd be lying on a table naked as a body can be in the operating room, being prepped by one of those nurses. And for reasons I do not to this day understand, she felt the need to call on the other four for assistance. So all of them were standing there while she shaved the area for the operation.

I don't know what you know about cardiac procedures like catheterization but the way to a man's heart is *not* through his stomach—it's actually nine or ten inches further south. This meant that the woman shaving me, and talking enthusiastically about the spell of lovely weather we were enjoying was moving various parts of me out of the way. Which, in other circumstances, may have been an interesting consideration, except that she was slathering shaving cream on my dainty delicates and swiping away with a straightedge razor within fractions of an inch from those very devices that have meant so much to me for so long.

The bevy of nurses began laughing. Now, they may have been laughing at her comments that we sure could use two inches of rain, or that her garden was so dry the beans were barely up out of the ground, or that her begonias were drooping and their buds were so small this year, it didn't hardly seem worthwhile keeping them around. Nonetheless it made me feel a trifle uncomfortable.

It didn't help that when I woke up in the recovery room hours later, someone had painted a happy face down there and a bunch of wise comments (like, "break a leg!") with iodine. The doctor said that nurses always do that to cheer up the patient. I'm not so sure.

USING YOUR HEAD

Any serious diet plan warns against shopping for groceries while you are hungry. Same with looking for babes. If you are desperate and you go looking for women, you are setting yourself up for some real problems. I know some of you are asking yourselves, "What's wrong with this Welsch guy? Why is he missing the most obvious place of all to look for women? Doesn't he get a newspaper out there in the Nebraska Sandhills? Is he an idiot or something? Why has he not yet said one single word about looking in the newspaper and then becoming a member of any one or several of the support groups listed under the paper's personals ads for love and sex addicts?"

How do I deal with this issue diplomatically? Do you like onion rings? I do. I love onion rings. How about eating all the onion rings you want, right now? All you want, all you can eat, on me. Okay. Enjoy that did you? Pretty good chow, huh? Now, here's another five-pound bucket of onion rings. Eat them all up. I'm just going to go ahead and order another bucket for supper. Bright and early tomorrow morning we can start off with another bucket, maybe this time with blue-cheese dip. We'll have more for lunch, if not before. And then we can munch away during the afternoon. And guess what's for supper?

You get the idea. Or if you don't, go ahead and go to a meeting for love and sex addicts and do your best. Give me a call when you recover. A kind of testimony about such indulgences comes to me from a friend and reader. When he sent me this story he probably wasn't thinking of it in terms of an explanation of why it may not be such a great idea to shop for a mate in a place for women whose hobby has become mating. But here it is, and I suggest you read it and think about it fairly seriously before you attend your first meeting of any support group for love and sex addicts, thinking to find yourself a life partner:

> Hi Roger,
>
> I have been reading your books about tractor restoration and have enjoyed reading them. In your books you talk about your love for the WC Allis tractors, which brought to mind something that happened at the family farm when I was a boy living at home.
>
> The Allis tractor was a good tractor for field work but I'll bet you never heard of using the WC for bull training! That's what I said—bull training.
>
> We milked cows and had a bull to take care of the cows when needed, if you know what I mean. Well this bull was the meanest one Dad had ever had, according to him. We had an old horse-drawn manure spreader in the cow yard and the bull would push it around the yard. He would pick

it up with his head just for something to do for excitement after the cows didn't want anything more to do with him. When Dad decided it was time to put the bull back in his pen, he would grab his pitchfork, go out in the barnyard and herd the bull into his pen.

Well, one day the bull didn't want to go to his pen. After Dad chased him around the yard a number of times, he'd had enough. Dad headed for the machine shed, got out the WC, and headed for the barnyard. He opened the gate and started chasing the bull with the tractor. The bull decided it was a nice day and went for a stroll down the lane to the 24-acre field.

Dad had reached the boiling point and was in hot pursuit with the WC in road gear! It wasn't long before the bull was tired and stopped running, but this was war! Every time the bull would stop, Dad would place the front end of the WC in the bull's backside, telling him the race was not over and continued all the way around the field. By the time the bull reached the gate to the barnyard, his tongue was hanging out and he was breathing rather heavy. The bull made a beeline for his pen.

The score was: Dad 1, the bull zero!

Now, Dad had the bull a few more years. Every time he wanted the bull in the pen he would go get the WC, set it by the gate and let it idle. The bull would go straight to his pen!

Sincerely,
John Fobian

LETTING GOD CHOOSE

Laura Schlessinger, the radio relationships-Nazi, says church is a good place to meet potential mates, but as usual, this self-righteous nut is so painfully wrong, she should be jailed for talking while under the influence of stupidity. Laura is also, as usual, her own best contradiction: she changed her own religion at least once. Thus, if her husband were anything but a simp who is addicted to her enormous wealth, and if he followed her advice, he would dump her because they are no longer religiously compatible. Religion is intensely serious stuff. It's okay if you both believe the same thing and never change, but what happens if religion is the fundamental building block of your relationship and one of you changes? Now where are you?

Linda and I are of different faiths. We've wrestled with the tough problem and sorted it out. The main issue is not whether one of us is right, but if one of us is wrong. If you embrace a religion that insists it and only it is right and that it has all of the truth always, you've got trouble no matter what you do. You're going to be lucky to keep a friend, much less a spouse. But if your religion or your personal understanding of it allows for the slightest possibility that you individually, or that your church collectively, doesn't know absolutely everything, then there is room for difference, the potential for understanding.

A fundamental part of both our faiths, Linda's and mine, is that we don't know everything. To me that seems obvious, but I see all around us people who insist that they really do know absolutely everything. In fact, it's the dumbest people we know who insist they are the only ones who are right. The smartest are the least certain, which includes Linda and me. Because we don't each know every- thing, Linda might know something I don't. And vice versa. This means that even if we have differences, that doesn't mean the other person is wrong. Or that we are always right.

Bars, taverns, lounges, and clubs are very bad places to find a potential mate. Remember how stupid you got the last time you went out cruising for babes and went to bars? Would you want to have anything to do with someone dumb enough to go out with someone as obnoxious as that? Uh-uh. This hunting ground works only for bride-for-a-night, catch-and-release adventures.

In the modern, cyber-world there is a lot of chatroom, email, cyber-sex stuff going on. Won't work. With luck like yours or mine, that airline attendant named Heidi who loves long walks on the beach, cooking fancy meals for two, warm cozy nights by the fireside, and exploring the limits of human sexuality is actually a cop named Bruno. And if that happens, it won't work out, even if he likes you.

Mom & Dad, You Do It

I was a graduate assistant teacher at the University of Nebraska back in the late 1950s, pretty well educated, married, fairly confident of my grasp of right and wrong, what works and what doesn't. I shared an office with a dozen other novice teacher-scholars, one of them a perfectly delightful young lady from Bolivia. She taught Spanish, I taught German. One day she was at her desk, opening her mail, and all at once this very quiet, sweet young lady sputtered to life, laughed, cried, trembled, giggled, shook her head.

I stepped over to see what was going on in her life to excite such a dramatic reaction. She showed me a photograph of a nice-looking young man and said, "This is going to be my husband when I go back home next year!"

"Wow, Wendy," I said, somewhat confused. "I didn't even know you were engaged to be married."

She shot me The Look as if to make a point of how stupid men can sometimes be (Note: Woman School is international) and said, "Well, silly, I wasn't engaged. My parents just picked him out for me this past month!"

It hit me like a concrete block. She was a victim of an arranged marriage. My lovely young friend was going to return to her backward nation where her parents had cruelly arranged for her to be put into the bed of a man she'd never so much as met, much less fallen in love with. Talk about barbaric! I was about to suggest that we could shave her head, disguise her as a Mexican field worker, and sneak her out of town and into the Spanish-speaking community. There she could, under an assumed identity, lead a life without such primitive coercion, eventually find her true love and marry him, as is appropriate among civilized, decent people.

She'd lived here long enough to know what I was about to say. She laughed, shook her head, and said gently, "Roger, the way you people do such things here is so sad, so stupid. You take two young people who don't even have the sense to drive well, who aren't capable of caring for a dog properly, and precisely when they are so soaked in hormones that they haven't the faintest notion what they are doing, you let them make the most important decision of their lives based on the dumbest conceivable emotion—love!"

Maybe Wendy had a point.

She continued: "My parents love me very much. They want the best for me. They will make sure this is a good man, able to care for me and our children, suitably educated and on his way to success in his career. They have met him and interviewed him. They have checked his family and his life so far. They have gone to see the home where he expects me to live. Will I love him? If my parents love him, there is an excellent chance that I will, too. If they are prepared to deliver to his bed their most precious possession—me!—then you can be sure they have considered everything very carefully. I will love him. He is so handsome. I will love him."

Last I heard, she did. And still does. On the other hand, I have divorced the woman I was married to at the time. Turned out we really weren't at all compatible. Our folks said they knew it all along. Moral of the story: Have your parents find a good woman for you. Of course, they may have to go to Bolivia.

OR A CHINESE RESTAURANT

Okay, so Nebraska is not exactly famous for its Oriental dining. Nonetheless, there are Chinese restaurants (mostly with waitresses named Lucille, Maxine, or LaVerne and busboys named Juan) and, like fine Chinese restaurants everywhere, the place mats are little paper thingies explaining the Chinese New Year and the arrangement of naming the years according to animals, which then determines your personality, compatibility, and criminal tendencies. I am not speaking here of your fortune cookie, a form of divination I find absolutely staggering in its ability to read its ingester.

> *The man's desire is for woman; but the woman's desire is for the desire of the man.*
>
> **—COLERIDGE, TABLE TALK**

To this day I have a cookie fortune taped above the very screen I am looking at at this very moment. It is so uncannily accurate, I can't help but look around me wondering if some little Chinese guy (or more optimistically, some luscious, seductive, quiet, eager-to-please woman who looks like Connie Chung) is lurking behind the bookcase over there in the corner observing my every move. It says, "Your sparkle never fades. You are always full of light."

Anyway, that's not what I'm talking about. I'm talking about the Chinese system of naming years. You look up the name of the year in which you are born and it will tell you exactly with whom you are compatible or incompatible. Using this ancient, venerable, mysteriously Oriental system you can flawlessly and seamlessly determine who to continue pursuing or evading simply by asking what year she was born.

Linda, for example, was born in 1954, which was a Year of the Horse, while I was born in 1936 and am, therefore, a Rat. If we examine the guidelines on the place mat I just lifted from the Hunan Restaurant in Grand Island last week, we see that The Rat is under no circumstances compatible with The Horse, and the one human being a Horse-year person should avoid having anything to do with is The Rat.

Never mind.

WITH FRIENDS LIKE THIS

I have never in my life been dumb enough to let friends line me up with a date. I can understand having a female relative or wife of a buddy or someone like that coming up with a date for me, but you'd have to be flat-out crazy stupid to let a male friend line you up with someone. I mean, jeez, think about it!

Twice in my life I joined in a cabal to set a buddy up, which is to say, I was not the dater or datee but the facilitator (or complicator). A bunch of us here in town once got to worrying about our pal, Co-op George, and his nonexistent love life. He openly and honestly confessed, after the fifth or sixth rum and Coke, that he was a virgin. He was maybe 35 years old, kind of goofy but thoroughly loveable, a really nice guy, if a trifle boring. We guys all liked him and figured that if we liked him, there must be some woman who would love him. As Woodrow said, quoting a word of wisdom from his own mother, "There's no pot so crooked that it can't find a lid." And we set our minds and efforts to finding a lid for Co-op George.

We did indeed find a woman whose desperation matched Co-op George's. She not only went out with Co-op George, according to George's somewhat confused reports, she relieved him of his burden and gave him a chance to taste for the first time the pleasures of the flesh. In this woman's case, that was quite a lot of flesh and, George admitted, a limited amount of pleasure.

I realize this is not much of a story, and in fact almost looks like a contradiction of my stated aversion to blind dates, but the thing is, George died two years later, not having so much as reached the age of forty. I don't know if our ministrations to his baser physical needs had anything at all to do with his early demise, but it seems entirely possible. The woman in question is still alive and kicking. Coincidence? I think not.

The second occasion in which I joined a campaign of seduction was perhaps safer but also less likely to succeed. I was a young faculty member at a small sectarian college. There was a particularly bright and mature student in the sciences, destined for great things. Like Co-op George, this guy was a complete, total, abject, unrelenting nerd. Not as boring, perhaps, as George, not as goofy, but not much of a catch, especially in terms of the furious social demands imposed by college life.

In this case, the male in question wasn't just flailing at shedding his unboinkativity, he had a designated object of his affection, a woman he most ardently hoped and prayed would be his very first boinkette. It was not the task of his friends simply to get him in bed with someone, anyone. He was moony-eyed googly over one particular coed. And he was not, like George, willing to settle for damn near anything warm and willing. No, this guy had set his sights on a campus beauty, a real prize for anyone. She was almost certainly going to marry someone rich, powerful, athletic, bright, sophisticated, and romantic. All of those things, in fact, that our young friend was not.

I imagine it was a breach of ethics for us to have anything to do with this, but our friend was such a good guy, his lust was so sweet and innocent, and the girl was so beautiful that we decided this was a challenge worth taking on. One faculty member loaned him her wonderful private swimming pool with underwater lights for the D-day effort. An English professor armed him and drilled him on romantic poetry so devastating we were certain no woman could resist it. I provided some incredibly elegant and aphrodisiacal strawberry wine I had made and aged in oak casks. The lad bought filets and we all worked with him on cooking them to absolute perfection. A music department prof put together an audiotape of the most romantic musical themes of all time to play softly in the background.

As you can imagine, the next Monday after this collective, carefully choreographed seduction, we were all absolutely panting to hear our young friend's account of the preliminaries, and, hopefully, the most intimate details of his conquest. He reported that the evening was a total bust. She drank the wine, ate the steaks, thanked him, and said she had to study for a midterm exam so she needed to be back at the sorority house early. That was it. Not even a peck on the cheek for all our efforts.

Actually, that wasn't all there was. It turned out later that she thought the whole thing was silly and contrived. She didn't like steak and preferred a hearty Bordeaux. She liked pop music, not classical. She didn't give him time to even get to the poetry. She told her friends that it was almost as if a committee of half-wits had put together some kind of plan.

Women can be so thoughtless, so cruel, so calculating.

MAIL-ORDER BRIDES

Not long ago I was stranded in a cabin far above the Arctic Circle for six months with absolutely nothing to do and I was finally driven to opening, even reading a disgusting magazine someone had left there years before. I think its title was *Penthouse* or something like that. You can be sure I'd never look at something like that under any other circumstances. Not me.

Anyway, in the back of this magazine, after all the articles about military law, civil liberties, and gourmet foods, behind the interviews with literary figures and art critics, well after the articles about sports and news, I was appalled to find an extensive section of small advertisements, many for mail-order brides from the Orient, former Soviet states, and South America. This is all right, I suppose, if you like ethnic types. Me, I don't even know if what they say about Oriental women is true.

Whatever the case, I looked at these ads fairly carefully. The women are gorgeous, and the little blurbs suggest they are compliant, eager, uninhibited, and desperate for love. I could see by their eyes that they were.

Then I remembered the time last year when I ordered a "genuine aquarium" stocked with "sea monkeys" that promised to "delight and entertain me hour after hour for many years to come." What I got was a plastic box about the size of a pack of cigarettes, an envelope with some fishy-smelling powder in it, and instructions on how to dump the powder into the plastic box and add salt water. A couple days later I could see some little bugs jerking around in the water, but they died pretty much totally a couple days later when the water turned green and started to smell real bad. This didn't strike me as at all entertaining for even minutes, much less "hour after hour for many years to come."

I have the feeling things would go pretty much the same if you ordered yourself up a Sasha, Ling-hoo, or Rosalinda from an advertisement in the back of a magazine.

A Best Bet Babe-ing Tip:
Kissin' Cousins!

I know what you're thinking. Okay, Rog, you keep telling us where not to find a woman. When are you going to get to the place where we should find a woman?

I have given you clues in the stuff I've told you so far, but if you are a typical male, you are way too oblivious to subtlety to have noticed. I have told you lots of stories about disasters in relationships and some unlikely examples of successes, but the most common example of a well-oiled, efficient, smooth, functioning, model relationship is Linda's and mine. So, I think we can conclude (don't listen to Linda on this) that we are a perfect couple.

But I'm no fool. I made it clear to Linda early on that I married every 22 years. I was married when I was 22, again when I was 44, and now, as I approach 66, I can only assume that I'll be looking around again. It's tradition. This means that I am not just mouthing a bunch of theoreticals here like some lame-brain "Doctor" Laura. It won't be long before I am going to be faced with some major mate shopping. I'm not just giving advice, I'm reviewing my *own* options for the very near future.

To tell you the truth, I'm not sure it's not divine intervention. I consider it a major sign of spiritual guidance that the answer to my own questions about finding the next Mrs. Welsch were answered, in a way, through the agency of Linda herself. (I should note that in response to the gasps of horror from women who are illegally reading this book aside, Linda is dealing very well with her pain in anticipating the approaching loss of her only husband to date. She puts on a brave face and says, "Great. I could use the break." We all know what she means.) In fact, I have some suspicions that Linda herself arranged for what is clearly a response to my search for a new spouse this coming summer: a Hotovy cousins reunion.

All her delicious Bohemian cousins will be gathering in one place, sort of like a female flea market, where I can easily compare and contrast, mix and match. This arrangement will save me the immense trouble of getting used to a whole new set of in-laws, unfamiliar ethnic food traditions, and extra-ethnic polka steps. In fact, Linda has offered to stick around for a brief transition period. She says she really can't afford to take more than five or six weeks because she has other things to do, another wonderfully brave gesture on her part. I am a trifle uneasy, on the other hand, about some comments she has made about hanging around even longer if it turns out she and the selectee cousin get to having too much fun.

If you are a typical American male, you are now thinking, "Hey, this Welsch guy is some kind of mover! No wonder he wrote the book. He is now moving very, very smoothly into a *ménage a trois* with two cousins! What a guy! Ol' Rog is my hero." Well, I'm even smarter than I look. See the section below on polygamy and ménages aux beaucoups. According to my research, this is not nearly the kind of fun you might think.

Also, I'm an old man. Two Bohemian girls in one household sounds to me like a cardiologist's dream. The last time Linda spent a day with one of her cousins she described the situation as "two dry pieces of wood looking for a match." I've given some thought to that metaphor. I've done what I could to put an attractive spin on it, and I've done some pretty adventurous imaginings, but the bottom line always comes out, "The old fat guy gets hurt." I look around: I'm the only old fat guy in the room.

CHAPTER 5

S EX

Love . . . sex . . . it's important to decide which.

—GEORGE SCHWELLE, *VISIONS*

Never do it outdoors.

CHAPTER 6

COURTSHIP
AND LOVE

It's a romantic comedy. You know . . . a fantasy.

—LINDA WELSCH

LOVE, *n.*

A temporary insanity curable by marriage or by removal of the patient from the influences under which he incurred the disorder. This disease, like caries and many other ailments, is prevalent only among civilized races living under artificial conditions; barbarous nations breathing pure air and eating simple food enjoy immunity from its ravages. It is sometimes fatal, but more frequently to the physician than to the patient.

—Ambrose Bierce, *Devil's Dictionary*

Right about here, things are going to start moving real fast, so try to keep up. The little bit of space between that last chapter and this one in actuality represents a billion light years. Toying and tinkering with love is just fine and relatively harmless, much in the same category as juggling running chainsaws or swimming naked in a tank full of piranhas. Now I am making an enormous leap to courtship and love, more akin to classical moral dilemmas like selling one's soul to the Devil or inviting two Jehovah's Witnesses who knock at your door to come in and chat.

Up to now we've been talking about fun and games; now we are going to get deadly serious. So cut out the giggling and try to pay attention.

You might think that there's nothing much new to be said about love and courtship, but I have every indication that either not enough has been said or not enough has soaked in. Web sites, e-mail, regular mail, conversations, discussions, shouting matches, and messages scratched on prison walls indicate that: 1) there are still a lot of questions about love and sex in this world, and 2) no one seems very satisfied with available answers.

For one thing, every man who falls in love figures he's the very first one who's ever done so. Hey, he's never been to Man School. What does he know? (Yes, and as usual, the woman who has been to Woman School knows all about this and is fully prepared to take total advantage of her educational edge.) A guy who has taken a date to the senior prom, done two slow dances, and has thumbed through his dad's *Playboy* collection thinks: 1) he is just about as sophisticated about the erotic arts as anyone possibly could be, and 2) that women know absolutely nothing about such things.

Part of the problem is that high school history classes are mostly taught by wrestling and track coaches who need one more course to fill out their schedules so they can collect full-time pay. I imagine that when the principal is working on this kind of problem, he thinks, "American history? Hell, anyone can teach American history. Give it to Bruno Testeroni, he can handle it." Bruno is going to teach history the miserable, dumb, boring way history is always taught in American schools. As Harry Truman once allegedly said, "The problem with history is that it's just one damn thing after another." Amen, Harry.

Real history is not only more interesting than that, it is also more instructive and entertaining. At this moment I am sitting where I've been sitting most of my life, right smack in the middle of the country, right smack in the middle of Nebraska. I'm a few miles from the Oregon Trail, the Pony Express Trail, the Mormon Trail, the Overland Trail, and probably a few other trails no one has bothered to name. And we all know that life on the trails was dangerous, miserable, lonely, and cheerless.

Well, that's not the way it was at all. That impression comes from people who: 1) are themselves cheerless, or 2) want to glorify ancestors who were no better at all than anyone else and probably a good deal worse. Many people went west on the trails often because they weren't doing very well or were on wanted posters where they had been. They were not courageous and progressive; they were dumb. They had no idea where they were going, or what it was like on the way, or what they would find when they got there.

They were also like us in that they knew how to have a good time. They liked their booze and they fooled around with their neighbors' wives—major problems, by the way, also among the Pilgrims at Plymouth. The most common cause of injury and death on the Oregon Trail was not Indian attack, or even disease or starvation but accidental gunshot wounds. These oafs were way too busy shooting themselves and each other to worry about the dreaded Injuns!

In the evenings they didn't all collapse in exhaustion, gather in a little circle, sing hymns and praise the Lord. Some did, but far more took a couple hits off the rum barrel, started tamping down the grass and dirt on some flat spot, and agitating for ol' Jim to get out his fiddle and start the dancing.

And listen to one of the most common songs of and about the cross-country trails:

"Don't you remember Sweet Betsy from Pike,

"Who crossed the wide mountains with her lover, Ike."

Lover? What about that pioneer sanctity of marriage? Nope, the song says it right there. This Betsy woman from Pike County, Pennsylvania (or Missouri, I can't remember which), was traveling across the nation with her lover.

But maybe they were just, well, uh, good friends?

"One day the old wagon came down with a crash,

"And out on the prairie fell all kinds of trash;

"A few little baby things done up with great care . . . "

Later verses do make an "honest woman" out of Sweet Betsy.

"This Pike County couple got married, of course."

The song then reveals that Betsy was also as modern as any member of the National Organization for Women.

"But Ike he grew jealous, obtained a divorce;

"Betsy quite satisfied gave out a shout,

"'Goodbye, you dumb lummox . . . I'm glad you backed out!'"

Is this kind of courtship and disunion just a figment of a song-writer's imagination? I don't think so. All you have to do is spend some time interviewing old-timers, the real fonts of wisdom and sources for historical truth in this country, to get the clear impression that things haven't changed one little bit.

THE FRONTIERS OF ROMANCE

A couple in their late nineties once stopped by Dannebrog to chat with me and they got to telling me their story—typical, tough pioneer fare. They had come over separately from their native Scandinavian countries with nothing. He worked as a hired hand on a Wisconsin farm, not far from where she wound up being a house-keeper and dairymaid. Eventually they started the process of court-ing and the time came when he asked The Big Question. He told me his exact words from over seventy years earlier: "Babe, I know I ain't all that good lookin' but I was wonderin' if you would marry me." He said she thought it over a minute or two and then said, "Well, you'll be out in the fields working most of the time anyway, so okay." Babe was standing right there and authenticated the story as true.

There are also hints from pioneer accounts that women were not always the pale and frail delicate flowers of the old Hollywood

Westerns but could be just as red-blooded then as now. Again, if we look a little longer and deeper at pioneer accounts, we begin to see a different history. One of my favorite stories was told to me by a woman who insisted that this actually happened to her grand-father, who was an itinerant house-hold-goods salesman in the pioneer West. He would travel from farmstead to farmstead

> *Love butters no parsnips*
> —MARK TWAIN

selling needles, pins, thread, pots, pans, and spices—the kinds of things a family might need but really couldn't afford to take the time to travel to town to get.

Well, he was out in the middle of nowhere, which could be said of almost anywhere in Nebraska, when a ferocious blizzard suddenly hit, and he knew he was in big trouble. With incredible good fortune he stumbled onto a sod-house farmstead, knocked at the door, and explained his plight. The farmer told him he was welcome to the modest shelter he and his wife could offer in their soddie, and even took the traveler's team out to the barn, where he bedded them down and fed them oats along-side his own animals.

Back at the tiny house, the storm-bound trio prepared for supper—much too flattering a term, as it turned out. The farmer's wife took a bowl of cottage cheese out of the cupboard, put it on the table, gave them each a spoon, and announced that this was it for the evening. The traveler had only gotten a good start, ladling maybe two or three spoonfuls of cottage cheese when the wife suddenly took the bowl and put it back into the cupboard, announcing that because that was all the food they had in the house, they would have to save the rest for tomorrow.

They got ready for bed, but all there was in that humble one-room shack was the one bed, so they all three got into it. The wife by the wall, the husband in the middle, the traveler on the outside, all on that same cornhusk mattress. In the middle of the night, there was suddenly this horrible racket that could be heard even over the roar of the storm and through the thick walls of the sod-house. The farmer jumped out of bed and said, "Good Lord, the horses are fighting out in the barn!" and went dashing out the door, through the deep snowdrifts outside the house to separate the horses and harnesses and all the mess out there in the barn.

After a second or two, the farmer's wife reached over and poked the traveler, saying, "Now's your chance," whereupon he got up and ate the rest of the cottage cheese.

If we were to assign an element of lustfulness in this historical and literary narrative to one of the protagonists in question, who exactly is the lustful initiator of the naughties in this little story? The tough and macho husband? The raunchy and worldly salesmen? Who then? Yep, that's right, the lady of the house!

In my files there is no end of bawdy pioneer stories along this same line. What it says to me is that if we are surprised to find that today's women are as sophisticated about love, sex, marriage, courtship, strategy, psychology, manipulation, trickery, or deception as any man . . . well, we just haven't read our history.

A WILY PREY

Just a few days ago a young lady of my acquaintance went through a painful breakup with her long-term boyfriend. I wasn't surprised to see the relationship dissolve, but I was surprised that there seemed to be no change in how things were working. The young man was with her precisely as much as he had been before they broke up. I mentioned this curiosity as casually as I could to the young lady and her response screamed "Woman School." She said, "I should have broken up with him a long time ago. Now he's nice to me."

Absence not only makes the heart grow fonder, it makes a man swallow harder. They know that. And now you do too. Not that there's anything you can do about it, but now you know.

Lovely Linda and I were about two months into our steamy courtship (it was during the summer, and in Nebraska in the summer even negotiations for a new coon hound can get steamy) when she decided things were moving too fast. I hadn't actually gotten to third base yet but I had sacrificed twice to right and dragged a bunt down the third base line that advanced the runner. Anyway, Linda told me that she thought she needed "more room" and that we should "have time to consider our situation" and suggested that maybe I take a cold shower and call her back in, oh, a month. And she left.

> The most common form of myopia is love.
>
> —GEORGE SCHWELLE, *VISIONS*

I got to thinking about this. And I said to myself, "I think you'e not being appreciated here. She wants more room? She wants some time? Well, fine and jimmy damn dandy! Let's give her some room and plenty of time. How about I just call you back around Halloween, Missie?"

I got to thinking some more, and I thought, "Time? Room? How about Thanksgiving? Would that be time enough for you, Linda Katherine Angela Hotovy? In fact, maybe I'll give you a call about Christmas. Or New Years. You want time and space? You're gonna have time and space. How about I just don't call at all. Maybe I'll wait for *you* to call *me*. How does that suit you, Miss Oh-So-Roomy-and-Timely?"

Whereupon I joined the Navy and went to war against the Japs. Well, not exactly, but close. I went on a weekend canoe trip. At least I didn't whimper and whine, which is probably what she wanted. I did tell her that sometimes Nebraska's rivers can be killers; utterly unpredictable cauldrons of seething foam and rock and that I might not be back.

Once again, however, I made the mistake of thinking. Never a good idea, thinking. During the long, long boring voyage of almost three full days I began to feel like a real cur, leaving Linda in pain and hurt like that. Maybe she was right, after all. She wasn't exactly rejecting me. So I thought maybe I'd call her at Christmas.

Or, what the hell, it's only a couple days earlier—Thanksgiving.

Or Halloween. You know, just a quick "Hello, how are you? Kinda miss you a little. And maybe we could have lunch. Or something."

Or because we'd both be working at the university, maybe I could just drop by her office and wave hi. Or invite her out to a drink. Something like that.

Or just call to let her know I had survived the savage challenge of Nebraska's Grand Canyon of the Niobrara River. Just a courtesy check-in to let her know I'm okay.

You know what happened. I called her the second that damn canoe hit the bank and we were back together by Tuesday. But the main thing is, I stuck by my guns and showed her she wasn't dealing with some kind of wuss who needs his mommy.

TRIED AND PROVEN TECHNIQUES

Whatever they tell you, believe me, honesty is not the best policy. It's like the old thing where they ask you, "Do you think I'm fat?" Next to "Why don't you just marry me?" that fat-question is the most dangerous thing a man faces, up to and including karaoke night in a small-town tavern. This is no place for honesty, nor do you want to lie too outrageously. When that question comes up, the best thing to do is to swerve your car into an oncoming semi or plunge your face into a plate of hot, *al dente* spaghetti. Anything to change the subject as dramatically and quickly as you possibly can.

There's an old joke about the old lawyer advising the young lawyer. He says, "The three most important things about being a successful attorney are sincerity, sincerity, and *sincerity*. And once you convince them of that, you can get away with almost anything." That may work with sincerity, but my experience tells me that no human males can fake sensitivity. Since we don't exactly know what sensitivity is to begin with, we can hardly imitate it, right?

Take me, for example. Lovely Linda came to me a shy, gentle maiden. She swears that she saved herself for our wedding night. Of course, she is also the one who says that all brides are virgins, so I have some question about exactly how far I can trust her declarations in such matters. No matter. She was a shy and timid, fragile flower, and I knew right from the beginning I was going to have to fake sincerity and sensitivity, no matter how difficult it might be.

I did some reading, watched about 15 minutes of an *Oprah* show on sensitivity, shaved, bought some new commercial deodorant (I usually just slap on some gin), and tried to think sensitive thoughts.

I read her some poetry, for one thing. I can recommend this highly because I think it worked for me. I would, however, *not* recommend that you read from a book of limericks or try to compose your own stuff. That's really saying something, coming from me. I once entered one of those song-writing contests in a magazine where all you have to do is send in one of your songs and a check for $25 and if you show promise, they'll publish your poetry in their daily publication *The World's Very Best Poetry, No Shit*: Acme Poetry and Planing Mill, Patterson N.J. To everyone's surprise but mine, they wrote back that I do indeed have promise and for another $50 they would throw my work into the basket for the Nobel Prize for Literature.

My submission on that occasion has been buried in the sands of time, but I do recall that I suggested it be set to a Calypso rhythm. One verse went,

> *And when we're old and wrinkled up,*
> *A burning love will still fill our cup;*
> *And even when, and after we die,*
> *We'll love each other up in the sky.*

The problem is that men in courtship seem to drift off into one particular area, generally deemed insensitive by most women, and it has an ugly habit of showing up in poetry. So can the homemade lyrics.

Anyway, I read Linda some verses from John G. Neihardt's *Bundle of Myrrh*, which he wrote about a hundred years ago and which was pretty much banned in the United States, and with good reason. This is steamy stuff. For one thing, Neihardt was very short and you know how short men are. He had something to prove, and he did it with passionate poetry.

An artist in Paris read this hot little book and decided then and there that this little guy was such a torrid package, she was going to marry him. She wrote to him, in Bancroft, Nebraska, from Paris, and told him to brace himself, because she was coming halfway around the world to marry him. He met her at the train station in Omaha with a marriage license in his pocket, they were married, and lived happily ever after. There's a moral there, although right now I can't for the life of me figure out what it could possibly be.

Anyway, reading Neihardt's poetry to a woman is for all the world like dropping diamonds one by one into her sloe gin fizz. After you've read stuff like this to her, it's not easy to argue you were just looking for someone to talk with.

WHERE TO GO, WHAT TO DO

First impressions are crucial. A first date is not so much a social situation as it is an audition. This woman isn't interested in what you are like at this point. She wants to know what you are capable of when you are really, really, really desperate. She has learned in Woman School that soon enough she will find out what you are really like. After all, you can keep up this fraud about courtship for only so long.

In today's world there are millions of choices about where to go and what to do on a first date. Men are generally not very good at making choices like this, because what they see as a good first social experience is not always what a woman sees. Look carefully at the chart below:

DON'Ts	DOs
Monster Truck Rally	*Parade of Homes kitchen tour
Snapping Turtle Fishing Tourney	*Shopping
Denver Broncos locker room open house	Wendy's Salad Bar Festival
Marilyn Chambers Film Festival	N.O.W. Self-Actualization Workshop
Prostate info seminar	*Rose Garden Clinic
Pep Boys Valve Grinding Gala	Healthy Hair Funorama
COPS fan club meeting	*Barry Manilow concert
Strong Man Free-for-All Face Smash	Wedding Planning Extravaganza
ZZ Top concert	Cake-decorating class
Rocky Mountain Oyster Pig Out	Cat Appreciation Day Ceremonies
Rattlesnake Round-Up and Fry *	Committed Couples Sensitivity and Awareness Weekend
Naked Trampoline Olympics	*Any fashion show other than lingerie
Skinny-dipping with your buddies*	Skinny dipping with her buddies
*especially not on a first date	*especially on a first date

Sometimes the choices between the items on this list are not always clear, the options not altogether discrete. For example, you might imagine that taking a date to a breast-examination demonstration would identify you to her as a sensitive guy who's willing to give serious thought to women's issues. Well, yes, if the demonstration is at a medical clinic, but not if it is at a Hooter's restaurant. Moreover, the likelihood of any woman being very enthusiastic about you going skinny-dipping with her friends is slim, but you know, some things are just worth trying no matter how unlikely they might be.

Don't give up entirely on that first column, however. Save it for possible evenings out after you are married, especially if you are trying to figure out ways to terminate the arrangement. Items in the first column—for example, the Marilyn Chambers Film Festival—could be approached as a possible test date to see just exactly how much fun this woman is going to be. The danger, of course, is that she is going to be way too much fun, for example, if she shows up on the screen as one of the participants in the movies' activities. And for some guys I know, even that wouldn't be all that bad a deal.

If you have something to say to her that you know for a fact is going to make her cry, take her to a really expensive restaurant to do it. I have found with Linda that if she has a bad experience in any particular place, she never wants to go there again. So, I try to generate arguments in expensive places and not so much as open my mouth at a McDonald's until we are well clear of the parking lot.

Break any bad news to a woman before she orders. Chances are, if she's really upset, she won't be able to eat much, which would be pretty nice considering your restricted budget. Some men I know wait until the food is at the table, the theory being that then she won't eat what she's ordered and there will be more for them. I guess it depends on what her menu preferences are.

YOUR PLACE OR MINE

When the time comes along, as you certainly hope it will, when you are ready to retreat from the public venue to a more comfortable and personal one, you have some options: her place or yours? Most men I know would be perfectly content with the hood of the car, but remember, this is early on in the relationship and we want to demonstrate an artificially elevated level of sensitivity (say the word slowly, over and over until you get it right). And, having read the chapter in the book on sex, you know about the indoor/outdoor thing.

Take a look around your place at the plastic garbage can behind the TV, full of empties, the refrigerator within easy reach of the couch, the duct tape on the mattress, the cardboard in the windows. Say hi to the dog sleeping in the bathroom and try to remember the last time you cleaned that toilet. No, that pine-tree auto freshener hanging from the ceiling fan does not count as ambience. The box of wooden

> *Love comes in at the eye.*
> **—YEATS**

matches on the kitchen counter, left over from the party earlier this year when you and your buddies were lighting farts, is not going to be seen by this new woman in your life in the same light as a scented candle. You have no problem with dishes in the sink, left over from breakfast three weeks ago, but you'd be surprised how women see little things like this. And if she spots that bean can with the spoon still in it from this morning's breakfast . . .

No, my friend, you do *not* want to take her to your place.

Now, how about hers? This too presents some hazards. Again, you'll be surprised to learn that those little towels in the bathroom—the ones with the kitties on them—are not for hand washing. And just once leave the toilet lid up, especially in *her* place! Yikes!

The top cover on the bed is called a "bedspread" and you lie neither on it nor beneath it. All you'll find to drink in the refrigerator is Chablis wine that is as exciting as tap water. And no, you don't use that glass for white wine. Don't even try to look in the bathroom cabinet or closet. I don't know what all that stuff is either.

One of the most interesting elements of this first visit to the lair of the prospective mate, male or female, is that it often involves food, the most intimate biological function we share next to, well, you know. While it's one thing to demonstrate your vulnerability by sharing a meal—you know, crap between your teeth, dumping gravy down your front, wine into her lap, drinking out of the finger bowl, ordering from a French menu and getting sixty-three packets of dry crackers instead of pork chops, that kind of thing—it is one huge step further to expose your most profound inadequacies by cooking the food yourself.

I don't care how inexperienced in the kitchen a woman is, she is born with a certain amount of inherent knowledge about food and cooking, or, lacking even that, she knows how to order food in, put it into different containers, and then convince a man that she cooked it herself. For example, I should have suspected something the first time I went to Linda's apartment and she served me a wonderful meal of roast duck, dumplings, sweet-and-sour cabbage, creamed asparagus, a French baguette, a fine salad with crumbled gorgonzola cheese in a light olive oil, apple pie, ice cream, and cappuccino coffee.

But when I looked in her refrigerator for an ice cube for my drink, there was nothing in there but an empty yogurt tub and two dried slices of cheap bologna. Did I care? Of course not. She was gorgeous. I mean, let's face it: Who cares who made the roast duck?

THE MENUS OF LOVE

Let's consider the practical reality of this strategy of feeding a prospective mate. I have made quite an issue about the differences between men and women but nowhere are those differences more pronounced than when it comes to what each species considers to be food and how they deal with its preparation and consumption. Here, according to extensive research from the Welsch Institute for Gender Difference Research is the perfect romantic meal:

The Woman's Ideal Courtship Meal
*(starred items are rated optional)
   Scented candles (sandalwood)
   Linen tablecloth and napkins
   Soft music (Tony Bennett, Frank Sinatra, or Barry Manilow)
   Solid silver utensils, crystal stemware, bone china service
   A light Chablis, Evian water with a half slice of lemon
   Tossed spinach salad with balsamic vinegar and *touch of light
      virgin olive oil
   Lightly buttered croissants with imported raspberry jelly
* (Raspberry sorbet to cleanse palate)
   Quartered artichoke hearts with hollandaise sauce
   Chicken breast in lightly spiced sauce
   Asparagus spears with unsalted butter
   (Lemon sorbet)
   Chocolate dipped strawberries, light sherry, latte coffee
* (Lime sorbet)
   Fireplace and a snuggly, fuzzy throw
   A rental movie with Molly Ringwald or Brad Pitt
   A long night in each other's arms, talking about love and this
      wonderful new relationship
   A tender kiss
   He combs her hair

A Man's Ideal Courtship Meal
* (Again, starred items are optional)
* Bourbon shooters
* A hand or two of strip draw-poker

* Cold 12-pack of Bud
* Big, thick, rare filet mignon, or pork chops, or burgers, or
    pork rinds
* Naked Ping-Pong
  Orgasm
* Stanley Cup Playoffs on ESPN
* Under the Quilts Hide-and-Seek
* Arnold Schwarzenegger movie
* Another orgasm
* Long night's sleep
* Late morning phone call to see if she got home okay while you
    were watching the Schwarzenegger movie

EATING HABITS OF THE AMERICAN MALE

There are reasons while the male military meal is called "mess" and why all men to this day prefer to eat off steel trays and with their fingers.

At noon today daughter Antonia watched me head resolutely into the kitchen and without hesitation make myself a peanut butter-butter-toast-lettuce-and-braunschweiger sandwich. With what I will interpret as admiration and respect, she asked, "Dad, how *do* you decide what to eat?"

I think Antonia's question is more of an answer than a query. My question would be, why would anyone *think* about what to eat? Eating and thinking are essentially mutually exclusive activities, at least in my world and that of most men I know and respect. You don't *think* about eating; you just *eat*. The reason I ate a peanut butter-butter-toast-lettuce-and-braunschweiger sandwich is that I *wanted* a peanut butter-butter-toast-lettuce-and-braunschweiger sandwich.

No, actually that's not it either, now that I think about it. A man's eating is not a philosophical issue, it's art. You know the old thing about the sculptor who explains his statue of a lovely naked woman (actually, I think it was a statue of David, but most men I know will understand this example better if I make it a naked woman) by saying that he simply chisels away everything of the block of marble that isn't the naked woman. I just went out to the kitchen and mentally eliminated everything in the cupboards and fridge that wasn't what I wanted to eat at that moment. And what I wound up with was a peanut butter-butter-toast-lettuce-and-braunschweiger sandwich. In another kitchen, or at another time, I might have wound up with bacon grease–laced raisins and popcorn. In fact, now that I think about bacon grease–laced raisins, I think I'll go to the house and see if we have the proper ingredients for that potentially culture-altering invention.

Last night was a fix-your-own supper evening. I had some stuffed grape leaves straight out of the can, Swiss cheese on whole-wheat toast, cold Bush's beans, and a half can of black olives. Linda was aghast; I was content.

CHAPTER 7

MARRIAGE: THE LAMB LYING DOWN WITH THE LION

Keep your eyes wide open before marriage, half shut afterwards.

—BEN FRANKLIN

The current American conventions of marriage are not the only forms of commitment on the face of this wide and wonderful world, nor are they the best. They are not more natural than other systems or ordained by divine forces. They are simply our own peculiar variations as opposed to other peculiar variations.

I have done some teaching, for example, in anthropology and all I need to do is lecture about 10 minutes on the Pawnee system of marriage and there's not an American, male or female, within earshot who doesn't wind up scratching his or her head, wondering what the hell the Anglo-Europeans were thinking of when they wiped out that perfectly wonderful arrangement and almost did in that perfectly wonderful people.

But this book is for the modern Western male, so I won't go into all those delightful permutations at the moment (buy me a glass of beer sometime and I'll make you drool). Read on and you will find some preliminary and scientific examinations of some possibilities. But for the moment, I'm going to explore instead the variations currently practiced in this society. As an old cowboy named Henry once told me, "Married? Yeah, sure, lot of nights. But no *days.*"

Bachelorhood

Bachelorhood is a condition much praised in its absence—and occasionally, mistakenly, reviled. Three of my married buddies and I were once up at the town tavern discussing an absent friend and his curious life arrangement. John has been "seeing" a perfectly lovely female friend for almost 25 years, but they have never enjoyed the sanctity of marriage, or so much as hinted at it.

ME: Can you imagine that? All that time dating without any formal arrangements. What's that all about? How can they live like that, without getting married and moving into one household? Obviously they love each other and are somehow committed to one another, so why not get married?

LUNCHBOX, WOODROW, LEROY: Yeah, hmmm, wow, what *do* you suppose that's all about?

ME: They might just as well be married. They go everywhere together, they're pretty much recognized as a couple.

LUNCHBOX, WOODROW, LEROY: Hmmm, yeah, right.

ME: I mean, how dumb is that anyway? It sure doesn't make any sense economically. He has his apartment, she has her house. That's a lot of extra expense. And there are lots of times when they don't see each other for days.

LUNCHBOX, WOODROW, LEROY: Right, yeah, hmmm.

ME: And her house is really spiffy with nice furniture, antiques, a well cared-for lawn, everything tidy and neat.

LUNCHBOX, WOODROW, LEROY: Uh . . . .

ME: John's place is a damn pit, stuff scattered all around. He keeps a huge plastic garbage can behind the TV so when he finishes a beer, he flips the empty over the screen, ricochets it off two walls, and wham! It drops into the recycling can.

LUNCHBOX, WOODROW, LEROY: [*Stare quietly, thoughtfully into partially empty beer mugs*]

ME: He drives all the way over to her place two or three times a week and maybe stays over, but keeps all his clothes and guns and *Playboy* magazines over at his place and has to drive back and forth. What an idiot.

LUNCHBOX: [*Begins to sob softly*]

ME: I mean, think of the money he could save if he moved in with her . . .

WOODROW: [*Bangs his head firmly but quietly against the table*]

ME: I mean, they're almost married anyway and . . .

LEROY: [*Stares at the ceiling and shakes his head slowly from side to side*]

ME: Sue, bring us another round over

here. And while you're at it, bring
along a Jack Daniels shooter for each
of us, too.

LEROY: Make that doubles.

WOODROW: Here's to John.

LUNCHBOX: We . . . are . . . such . . . idiots.

An important point to remember in the early stages of courtship is to take full advantage of whatever a woman finds attractive about you. Is she drawn to you because you are a rugged outdoorsman? An avid reader? Because you are easygoing and undemanding? Independent and strong? Be that, and enjoy her attention and approval, because once you are married, those are precisely the features about you she will find obnoxious. About a year into any serious commitment you will find that this woman who has taken you on as a fixer-upper project is annoyed, and then disgusted by your insufficient couth (formerly "rugged outdoorsman"), sloth ("avid reader"), sloppiness ("easygoing and undemanding"), inattentiveness and general disregard for her needs and desires ("independent and strong").

I recently discovered that the pattern of logic/illogic in this matter continues in a direction utterly unpredictable by the normal male mind. You might think, being a male, that what she really wanted, probably, was not what you were. Maybe the opposite.

You would be wrong. When you've spent as much time around as many women as I have, you will find that you are always wrong. Even when Precious Moments agrees with you, as bizarre as it may seem, you are wrong. It is true that while there may or may not be a sound if a tree falls in the forest and there is no one around to witness the crash, a man, alone on a desert island or abandoned on the Greenland ice cap somewhere north of Qaanaaq, is wrong, whether anyone is there to disagree with him or not.

Back to the case study in question. Lovely Linda recently had reason to visit a man's home for business purposes. (That's what she said anyway, and I believe her.) She came home all agush about this guy because, you guessed it, his house was cluttered with books; his hair was wild and unkempt; he needed a shave; he was taking on way more projects than he had time, energy, or resources for; and he ran around with a bunch of wild-ass writers and professors. The same wild-ass writers and professors, in fact, referred to as derelict no-goods in some previous conversations she had with me.

You know me, the one who is a slob because I have books scattered around the house and don't comb my hair. Mostly because I never finish what I start and start more than I can ever finish. That guy. Me. Or the other guy. Depending on whether the question is approval or disapproval.

There is no male response or solution for this dilemma. Just shut up, swallow hard, and remember your wedding vows, which side your bread is buttered on, the hand that feeds you, what's warm, soft, and comforting, how bad your buddies smell when you camp out with them.

CELIBACY

Bachelorhood is not the same thing, therefore, as celibacy. Even that alternative has its advantages. As the late and very much lamented Bert Evans once said to me, "Abstinence isn't much, but it's better than nothing." My most remarkable brush with this form of living came quite unexpectedly when I was lecturing at a very prominent Catholic university. I gave my afternoon speech and was looking forward to a nice, quiet, solitary evening meal in this fairly cosmopolitan city before my evening presentation when the university official in charge of herding me around said, to my dismay, "The Jesuit fathers have asked that you join them for the evening meal. I hope that's okay. Father Joseph will be meeting you at my office in about 10 minutes."

I am generally a courteous guy, so I exercised diplomacy, smiled weakly, nodded, and began to gird my loins for an ecclesiastic evening of monastic dreariness. Just what I wanted: a meal in the silence of a bunch of monks. I imagined cold gruel and warm water drawn from the creek in leather buckets. Of course we would eat in prayerful silence.

I was sitting in the lady's office for only a minute or two when a dude (I use the word advisedly) came shambling in wearing jeans, a Def Leppard T-shirt, and sockless sandals. Another superannuated career student hippie, I assumed. The lady in charge of me smiled and said, "Roger, this is Father Joseph."

We ambled across the campus, making small talk about my field of folklore and the campus and the town and wound up on the porch of a large but unimposing frame house at the edge of the campus. "Here we are," Father Joseph said, and motioned me through the door. We had just cleared the threshold when he said, "Would you care for a pre-dinner drink? Or two?"

As if I weren't already surprised enough, the next exchange left me slack-jawed and glassy-eyed:

ME:	Sure, I'll have a little nip. What do you have?
FATHER JOSEPH:	What do you want?
ME:	What do you have?
FATHER JOSEPH:	What do you want?
ME:	[*Slyly, knowing the chances of these guys having really good stuff was slim*] Uh, okay, single-malt scotch.
FATHER JOSEPH:	[*Placidly*] What brand?

And he opened the hall closet just inside the front door to reveal as fine a selection of excellent drink as I have ever seen . . . Boodles Gin, Stoli Vodka, Wild Turkey Rye, Knob Creek Bourbon, French brandies, German Kirschwasser, absinthe, grappa, and aquavit. You name it, they had it.

Still reeling from the theological revisions my mind was struggling with, I joined a bunch of other casually dressed, glass-toting guys in another room. They were telling jokes. Like this one: St. Peter and Jesus are standing at the Pearly Gates watching this old, old guy struggling his way up the stairway to heaven. When he finally reaches the gates, St. Peter greets him, "Hello, Old Timer, welcome to heaven. What did you do during your time on earth?" And the old guy says, "I was a humble woodworker, but nonetheless enjoyed a blessed life."

"Any family?" St. Pete asked. "Well, yes, and no," the old man said. "I kind of had a son, but not actually a son at all. I loved him like a son, but he wasn't exactly a human being, and . . ."

By this time Jesus was very agitated and stepped forward, gasping, "Father, is it you? Father? Father?" The old man's eyes lit up, and he looked at Jesus, saying, "Pinocchio?"

Supper was served. Wonderful steaks right off the grill, baked potatoes with an incredible sour cream sauce that turned out to be the specialty of one of the other Jesuit fathers in the house, homemade bread, cigars, more brandy.

As I left this remarkable setting, I hinted at my Protestant amazement at this brotherhood—not so much its religion as its honest civility. Father Joseph suggested that any time I was in town and looking for some good company, food, and drink, I should just drop by. Someone would always be around. And he said, "Because your wife is Catholic, she'll figure you're in safe company and never give you any trouble about coming home late. Or not at all."

Moral: Abstinence is not all bad. And maybe devotion to God does not require misery.

LIVING TOGETHER

This arrangement is increasingly popular and has some merit. Before one becomes hopelessly ensnarled legally and emotionally with a woman, one could argue that it would be better to do a test drive and get some idea of exactly what sort of adjustments might have to be made in case the lease arrangement turns into rent-to-buy. On the other hand, there are some problems here that any male needs to think about.

For example, the words "How about let's move in together?" have entirely different connotations for women than for men. When a man utters this sentence, he imagines it means something like, "I could really use some help with my laundry and sometimes if I were just staying with you, I could have another beer or two, do a little naughty-wiggle, and not have to drive anywhere. And then you could fix me a little breakfast before you drive off to work in the morning."

> *I was married once—in San Francisco. I haven't seen her for many years. The great earthquake and fire in 1906 destroyed the marriage certificate. There's no legal proof. Which proves that earthquakes aren't all bad.*
>
> **—W.C. FIELDS**

A woman hears the same six words as meaning something like "I'm trying to get together the money for a diamond and in the meantime how about you helping me figure out how to sort laundry and live without a dog?"

Moreover, a man and woman in this kind of situation aren't really going to get an idea of whether the other person is compatible or not. A man who has never picked up a beer can or his own underwear once in his life is quite likely to do that for at least the first few weeks, or even months, of a communal living situation. There is no chance whatsoever of him doing that once vows have been exchanged. I mean, jeez, why would he?

Nor are women any more honest at this stage. I recall with some pain the first few times I brought Lovely Linda to my old log cabin down along the beautiful Middle Loup River of central

Nebraska. It's not as if I hadn't put some effort into getting set for her visit. I swept the dead flies and some larger organisms (possums, coons, bullsnakes—dead and alive) out of the house, put fresh toilet paper into the outhouse, picked up most of the empties off the porch, and put new sheets on the bed and burned the old ones (risking a citation from the EPA in doing so).

There was an element of fraud in that I gave the impression I was always such a fancy-Dan, nicky-picky Mr. Neatness, but Linda was not without her own guilt in this matter. I distinctly recall her saying things like, "Oh Rog, look at that cute spider! Never saw one that big. Why don't you take away the rabbit it just murdered and hack it apart with a machete?" And "Do I mind walking fifty yards to an outhouse in the middle of the night with a kerosene lantern? Of course not. I enjoy the night sounds and the rumblings of whatever it is that lives down there under the floor of the privy. What are you guessing that might be, by the way?"

Problem is, living together isn't even remotely like being married—until maybe the fifth or sixth year. About that time you wind up having all the worst parts of living together along with all the worst parts of being married. By that time you should have made up your mind. Marry or move on. Anyone who has children in this interim, temporary, ad hoc arrangement should serve time in prison.

LIVING TOGETHER APART

Actually, if culture functioned with any kind of logic at all, we would live together before we got married—*but not after!* The most successful cultures in the world have systems precisely along these lines. You hook up with the babe of your dreams, and then you get the hell out of there. She's yours, so now it's time to go hunt up some food for the family. Be back in about two months. Or go pick a fight with the tribe over the hill, where there are almost certainly a bunch of young guys looking for a reason to get out of the house, and women who figured out about three weeks into this marriage what dirty laundry looks like and are more than ready for a break too.

I once saw an interview with an elderly couple who got married many years before and bought two separate, identical houses, side by side. The husband lived in one, the wife in the other. They had a great time. They watched whatever they wanted on TV. She had a chenille bedspread; he slept in an army surplus sleeping bag. He had a dog; she had a cat. She bought figurines; he farted whenever he wanted to. Every evening they got together for supper and sometimes watched TV together, except for those evenings when she watched *Touched by an Angel* and he watched *BattleBots*.

> *Bigamy is having one wife too many. Monogamy is the same.*
> —OSCAR WILDE

The interview was meant to be funny. Boy, the interviewer seemed to be saying, aren't these old geezers peculiar? That night in bed I cried myself quietly to sleep.

Let's just note that while there is a word for commitment, there's none for dis-commitment. Think about it.

This could be a uniquely American problem. I was once visiting a perfectly wonderful, elderly couple in Newcastle, England. They were not only married for a lifetime, it was clear that they loved each other every moment of that lifetime, maybe even more late in life than they had earlier. I think I got a brief hint of how that relationship had thrived.

We were getting ready for an evening and I pretty much figured we were going to do what we had the other several evenings I had spent with them. We'd have a very nice supper, some conversation, and then about 9:00 P.M. the gentleman and I walked the half mile or so to his club, which is a sort of private tavern where we sat around, drank beer, laughed and talked with his friends until the place closed about 10:30 P.M. Then we walked back to his home where his lovely wife had prepared a small, hot pastry and some tea for us all before we retired for the night.

Very civilized, I thought.

As the hour approached for the mister and me to head out the door and up the hill to the club, he smiled, held up his finger, and said, "Now, I have an idea. Instead of going to the club tonight, Roger, why don't we just stay here in front of the fire and chat in the quiet and calm instead of in all that noise and smoke up there?" I had the feeling that what he was suggesting was in part an effort to let his wife enjoy our company too, to make it possible for her to chat with us, to have some company, to not be left out of the evening's fun.

Quite quickly and firmly the woman said, "Now, look here. I get only an hour a day when I have the peace and quiet of this house to myself, when I can do what I want, listen to my own music, watch my own shows on the telly, sit with the cat and think. You are *not* going to take that away from me, even for one night. You just get your coats, you two. Go out that door. Go to your stinky, loud club, laugh with your friends, and leave me alone!"

Yes, she was mostly laughing and giving us permission to go ahead and spend the evening with pints of wonderful, deep brown ales and lagers, to laugh at bawdy jokes, to discuss the day's football scores, but there was also enough honest truth in what she said that I've never forgotten it. We were walking. We weren't going to get into any trouble. We were together, and there weren't any women involved. We were with friends and there was no danger to life and limb.

When we came home, she was glad to see us, and we were glad to see her. A lot of American couples could learn something from those folks, huh?

A CLASH OF SENSITIVITIES

Again, rely on the proven rather than attempting the clever, especially if you are thinking up the new ideas on your own. What most men think are really neat ideas—hand fishing for catfish, lighting farts, stretching Saran wrap over a toilet under the toilet seat, are often not well received by women. In my own case, I tried to demonstrate my intense compassion for the animal world, an area I know Linda considered very important, by showing her how I put the little worms from the bottom of tequila bottles out in my bird feeder, thus providing the occasional lucky sparrow with one hell of a Christmas treat.

Far from considering this a demonstration of sensitivity, she insisted it was an example of insensitivity. I know pretty clearly what I was thinking in this process, and I think I have a fairly good notion of what the sparrow might have been thinking, but I cannot for the life of me come up with even the faintest idea of what Linda might have objected to in this process.

Using animals and wildlife as a vehicle for demonstrating your sensitivity to a woman can be a risky tightrope to walk. We've had the wonderful distinction over the past couple years of having a mountain lion take up residence in the woods along the river that borders the southern side of our mid-Nebraska farm. Although mountain lions aren't exactly cute and cuddly, I figured they *are* wildlife. The gun-happy half-wits around here are all fired up about the possibility of killing this big cat (and already did kill one just 12 miles from here), so the animal is hunted, harassed and endangered. Just the thing for Roger Sensitivity to champion and gain some points with his wife, right?

Well, in the middle of one discussion the trigger boys noted that lions have attacked and killed people and are, therefore, a dangerous neighbor. I had done my homework so I responded there have been no attacks in Nebraska, ever, and that even in Colorado the handful of attacks were against children and small women. Thus, I added, using my superior education, research, and sensitivity, all we really need to do is "breed an extra kid or two per family and feed our women more desserts."

Linda did not interpret this as a particularly strong demonstration of sensitivity on my part. It turns out that the factors of: 1) children being eaten, and 2) fat girls are not good elements of any male exercise in sensitivity, outweigh any threats to furry wildlife.

A WEIGHTY PROBLEM

In fact, the topic of weight control is *never* a direction a man should take up with *any* woman, no matter what the circumstances. As far as I can tell, there is for each and every woman a range of about two and a half ounces for what she would be happy with as her perfect weight. Even a variation of one ounce above that is perceived by her as overweight, and thus, any references whatsoever to weight will be interpreted as a personal insult directed like an arrow to her heart. One ounce below, you would think, therefore, would be flattering. No. Just take my word for it, no.

The area of weight and body image is a veritable minefield for any male, no matter how hard he is working at being sensitive. A man, trying to be sensitive, might, for example, hear his wife bemoan the fact that she weighs two pounds more than she did when she was in high school and how ugly she is and how she hates it and how she wants to do something about it. And so, this hapless but hopeful guy makes a point of going to the local Weight Watchers office and buys her a book of gift certificates for a year's worth of weight control visits for Christmas.

As good an idea as this might seem on the surface, it will not make her happy. In fact, she will cry and slam the door and maybe even go outside and cry. You'll sleep on the couch for weeks. How could you be so thoughtless and cruel? You can't answer that, of course, because you have no idea how you could be that thoughtless and cruel.

Linda worries about her weight. All women worry about their weight. But I think Linda is a lovely woman, and after all, I'm not quite the Adonis I was when we first met either. Twenty years not only take a lot out of a man, they put a lot onto a man. Anyway, Linda and I were once driving about 60 miles away from here to pick up a load of frozen meat for our freezer. It was a hot, August day, but it wasn't far so we hoped that the meat would be fine during the one-hour return trip. On our trip out, Linda talked about how she had to get back on her exercise program, and cut back on eating between meals, and cook more nutritionally light foods for us both, and how she wished she were back at her prime weight.

I was trying to tell her that I love her no matter what—certainly no less because she weighs more than she did when we first met, that she is beautiful no matter what, that her most valuable beauty is within—all things that are true. As if on cue, I could hear just faintly over our radio a song playing that seemed to be a heaven-sent message to reinforce my *sensitive* reassurances. It was the group Queen singing—I turned the radio up, confident that Linda would find the lyrics reassuring:

Oh, won't you take me home tonight?
Oh, down beside your red firelight?
Oh, won't you let it all hang out?
Fat-bottomed girls, you make the rockin' world go 'round!

Well, so much for trying to be encouraging. She didn't say another word to me all the way home. And that meat? It was so cold in the truck on the drive home through the Nebraska heat it stayed frozen, all right.

Stay away from any discussions about weight. Just nod and listen.

MORE SEX

By now you've probably noticed that I have been stuttering around about courtship and avoiding sex. Thing is, men love to joke about sex but they really don't feel very comfortable talking seriously about it. Sex has to be just about the most embarrassing thing a man ever does in his life, next to going into a grocery store and buying feminine hygiene products, which a man sometimes has to do if he has any plans to get any sex, in which case he'll probably do it.

Our sample of target-market readers at this point in the book complained that I had perhaps given short shrift to sex in the previous chapter. Well, okay, but in all honesty, I told you pretty much everything I know about sex, and Linda says she'll back me up on that. I'm not going to go into much more detail here because I doubt that I need to. Sex outdoors *is* a bad idea, unless you're a fly. In which case, sex could be seen as a great opportunity. Same with hammocks and canoes.

I guess I could offer some more helpful hints about sex, because everyone seems to be so baffled about it. At least, the men I know are baffled about it. Gents, the thing is, women expect love, sex, and romance to have some kind of focus. You're supposed to have given it some thought, and then devote some attention and energy to it, as inefficient as that might seem to you. I can guarantee you that you are headed for trouble if your sex life takes place mostly during halftimes. And take it from me, you are in even worse shape if it's during time-outs, between baskets, or during slow play. You need more help than I'm going to be able to give you.

I guess that's about all I have to say about sex. In fact, Linda says I've said more than enough already. But I'm not through with canoes, and if you think about it, sex can be a lot like a canoe, which is probably why it's a good idea not to think too much about it.

A New System for Stabilizing American Relationships

I am not simply a theoretician. I'm a practical guy with practical solutions. I have, therefore, approached several members of Congress about starting a program for stabilizing American relationships. I believe we can develop stronger American marriages and relationships if we pretest couples. If they can't get through these Trials of Aphrodite, we can save them a lot of years of agony trying to make it when it's clear they aren't going to survive no matter how long they work at it. On the other hand, if they can make it through this gauntlet, they can survive anything.

The following are only suggestions. I am confident that others have plenty of experiences that might lend themselves better to testing the true mettle of a prospective couple.

THE TRIALS OF APHRODITE

- Take a trip together, preferably getting lost at least once.
- Each person of the couple must at some point be ill in the presence of the other.
- Attend at least three weddings, at least one with each set of in-laws (in some families, the more revealing and frequent alternative for this trial would be a funeral, or better yet, a reading of a will. This should demonstrate the psyche of any family in rich detail).
- Baby-sit together, for at least 24 hours. First an infant, then a toddler, some multiple children of mixed age, and finally a preteen.
- Attend each other's family Christmas or perhaps a reunion.
- Split $1,000, $500 to each, and a week later discuss where it went.
- Balance the other's checking account for a period of not less than two months.
- Share living quarters during a power outage of not less than 24 hours.
- Take a canoe trip, sharing a canoe. No fair being in separate canoes. Anyone can do that.

• Introduce your prospective partner to all of your closest friends and spend four hours in a tavern, lounge, or party together. Both sets of friends. Together. In the same place. It might be a good idea to alert your local law enforcement agencies before you set up this particular trial.

I know that it's possible for people to fake their way through some, even most, of the above trials, but not all. For example, Linda and I first spent time together at my wonderful and rustic nineteenth-century log house down in the woods by the river. It's a grand place—quiet, peaceful, rustic—no distractions like television, telephone, electricity, plumbing, air conditioning, heat, or running water. Linda thought it was a wonderful place. She loved the coyotes howling outside the door at night, the buzz of the bees, the hooting of the owls, and the feeling of being close to nature. At least, that's what she said. After we were married, we never again overnighted at the cabin. I'm not even sure it's still down there.

THE MORE, THE MARRIEDER

Polygamy is a lot like bungee jumping in that it sounds like a lot more fun in theory than practice. As usual, the ultimate cynic, Ambrose Bierce, captured the spirit of the problem when he defined polygamy: "A house of atonement, or expiatory chapel, fitted with several stools of repentance, as distinguished from monogamy, which has but one." Recently there has been a lot in the news about some idiots in Utah who have herds of wives. (Actually, the word for a group of wives is not "herd," or for that matter even "harem," which is the romantical and Arabic term. The official Western measure is a *peck* of wives.) One guy in particular has been making the rounds of television interview shows with his peck of wives, mostly trying to explain away the fact that they were all underage when he performed the initial connubial boink.

The only sensible thing I have heard this clown say so far is that he supports them by sending them all out into the streets to sell magazines door to door. That makes a lot of sense. It not only results in income but gets them out of the house. Moreover, any woman stupid enough to buy into this kind of exploitation deserves exactly what she gets (although there is some substantial evidence that it is not always a choice, in which the man in question is little more than an unconventional pimp).

Consider for a moment the implications of the rest of this bozo's life scheme. Have you ever lived in a household with a teenage woman? I think of my buddy John Carter's assessment upon looking at my gorgeous teenage daughter, Antonia: "Rog, she's pretty cute from a distance. Sort of like a badger." And he didn't have to live with her. It's hell, plain and simple.

If a grown woman is just about the most inexplicable vexation in the world, no grown woman comes anywhere close to an adolescent human female. (I don't know why but I am somehow reminded of my favorite biblical passage, from the Song of Solomon, of course: "Who is she that looketh forth as the morning—Fair as the moon, Clear as the sun, And terrible as an army with banners?")

I have three daughters. I know what I'm talking about. Now imagine *marrying* a teenager. Imagine marrying two. No, make that three. Aw, what the hell, make it six, or nine.

If this kind of self-torture is too much for you, let's start easy, with something that is minor in comparison. Imagine glowing embers being jammed up under your fingernails, and then . . . nah, that's still too easy compared to marrying multiple teenagers. Imagine getting real sick and your doctor tells you that for the rest of your life you won't be able to eat anything—nothing at all—but tapioca. Nope, still too low on the pain scale. Okay, here it comes: imagine being stranded on a desert island for fifty years with a television set that shows only one channel, and it's the Lifetime channel.

Now imagine something ten billion times worse. Something almost as bad as being married to a teenager. Now multiply that by however many wives this poor benighted half-wit in Utah has. Going to hell? Don't be silly. This guy has created his own hell. If Satan's realm has bachelor's quarters, this guy is going to buy express tickets to get to them, and pay the price of the ticket with pleasure. Before I am misunderstood here, let me repeat a line of text from above: any woman stupid enough to buy into this kind of exploitation deserves exactly what she gets.

Still, the dreams persist, don't they? On a couple occasions I have mentioned to Linda when she complains about how much she has to do around here that maybe we need another wife to take some of the strain off of her, um, shoulders. Early in our marriage she would shoot me a nasty look or give me The Sigh, and I would laugh it off. But lately she's been saying, "Okay." Just like that: okay. And the time between my suggesting it and her okay is getting shorter and shorter. Why do I suspect something here? Any of you polygamists who can contribute to my thoughts about this are welcome to write me in care of the publisher. But not in care of Linda, please.

FOOLIN' AROUND

While women love to be surprised at Christmas, anniversaries, birthdays, or Mother's Day, etc., it is generally acknowledged that they tend not to be very enthusiastic, Linda tells me, about being surprised to find that you are visiting someone else's bed. Before any women who are reading this book without authorization get too huffy, I want to note that every single thing I say about this topic applies equally to women. In fact, I know more women who fool around than men. And I have, in my life, known one woman who had the gall to suggest that because of a long history of male infidelity, it was now her turn to even the score. Her husband should, in her estimation, remain totally faithful to her, while she exercised the sexual freedom which, according to her, all women are endowed by God, to sleep with whomsoever they wished. (She was very quickly without a husband, you can bet!) That's a quick double-standard path to spinsterdom.

When the opportunity presents itself, men often and suddenly think it might be perfectly logical to relieve their tensions, without burdening their wives with the problem. Not long ago during a counseling session, one of my patients (well, okay, it was up at the tavern, and it was a buddy spilling his guts) told me a woman had been flirting with him, and he was thinking . . . you know, he was thinking.

Marriage is a desperate thing.
—JOHN SELDEN

But he was somewhat concerned about what his wife might think should she find out what was going on. He presented his case very effectively to me and he wondered if it would work with his wife. "Rog," he said with heartfelt sensitivity, "you wouldn't be unhappy if I called you up some day and said, I'm not going to be able to go fishing with you this weekend because I'm going with Mel, would you? I mean, you wouldn't care, right? You'd probably just say, Sure, buddy, just let me know if and when you want to go out and drown a worm together some other time. I mean, you wouldn't start huffing and puffing and threatening never to go fishing with me again. That's just not what men do!"

"Right," I said. "And you sure wouldn't be unhappy if I called you up and said I was going hunting this weekend with Dave, right?"

"Nope, sure wouldn't."

"In fact, if I asked if we could use your blind, you'd have no problem with that either."

"Nope. Help yourself."

"And if Dave needed to borrow your 12-gauge?"

"Well, I mean, you know, I kinda hate to lend out my guns, but well, yeah, okay, I suppose if you asked, and it was Dave."

"And we'd probably be more than welcome to use your dog, Birdboy, right?"

"My dog?"

"Yeah, Birdboy, your Lab. We'd need a retriever, since we're going hunting and all. That sure wouldn't be a problem for you, would it?"

"My dog? Well jeez, Rog, I mean it was one thing to go hunting with Dave, and to use my blind, and even borrow my shotgun, but Birdboy. Man, Rog, you're really asking a lot here now. I just don't know. When it was just the blind, well—but wow, Birdboy."

See what I'm getting at? It's not just a matter of who's doing the borrowing, but just exactly what equipment is being put into use by the third party.

I once asked a friend of mine whose wife had just thrown him out if he had perhaps aroused her anger by his own actions. "Have you been fooling around with other women?" I asked.

"No more'n natural," he said, without a hint of irony.

"Has she been fooling around?" I continued. "Is there maybe another man?"

"Well, for Pete's sake," he sputtered. "*That* sure as hell wouldn't be natural!"

Most folks I know, men and women, eventually come to consider the fun of foolin' around to be but a small investment for the almost inevitable eventual harvest of a mountain of trouble. Before you consider this as an alternative lifestyle, you may want to check with your spouse, but not when he or she is loading a weapon. I'm not smart or educated enough to understand entirely why that is the case, but it pretty much seems to be the way things are.

I JUST DON'T WANT TO KNOW
WHAT THEY DO FOR FUN

I have written elsewhere about homosexual unions, but in case you've been too cheap or henpecked to get any of my other books, let me tell this one again. It bears retelling because it is absolutely soaked through with meaning like those last three Frosted Flakes floating in milk at the bottom of the bowl that time your wife went to visit her mother in Nebraska, and you didn't do the dishes for sixteen days.

Linda and I were talking recently about a crusade by a pack of self-righteous Nebraska super-Christians to persecute homosexuals under the guise of protecting marriage. (I don't know about you, but homosexuals don't have a single thing to do with *our* marriage, much less *threaten* it! But then, I don't know the exact nature of the marriages of these folks who feel so threatened.) There was the usual hypocrisy about loving the sinner and hating the sin, but this dishonesty was, like most lynchings, little more than another example of people who aren't up to managing their own lives trying to manage someone else's.

Despite my mind-your-own-business approach to such things, I was admitting to Linda that I have a really hard time imagining living like that. Probably because I'm a man, I said, it's harder for me to understand doing it with another man, but even lesbianism escapes me. Linda thought about this for a moment and then said, "Yeah, Rog, I agree. It really is hard to imagine coming home to someone who smells good. And doesn't need a shave. And whose clothes you can wear. And who knows how to sort laundry. And knows how to cook. And leaves the toilet seat down. Whose friends don't track mud into the house. And who loves a good sensitive movie. And who likes cats. Someone who I could watch Oprah with. And someone who picks up her own underwear. And someone. . . ."

That went on for about two and a half days until I finally said I had something to do up at Stromp's salvage yard and disappeared with a box of tools, a cooler of beer, and my buddies Lunchbox and Woodrow. There's such a thing in marriage as too much agreeing, I think.

In short, I guess homosexuality is okay but just don't overdo it with the interior decorating.

BORING!

We live in a small village in the middle of Nebraska. I guess you could call life here boring. I don't think it is, but some people might. I think the life I see in cities is boring, but that's because I prefer life out here. Our local television news in the evening runs pretty much to things like a report on the new tires just acquired for the senior citizen minibus over in Hastings, or the repaving project on the highway between here and Ord, or maybe the retirement of a minister who has served the same church for almost thirty years. I guess that's boring news.

Occasionally we get to Lincoln, our state capital, or Omaha, the closest thing we have to a real city. Sometimes we even travel to Chicago, New York, or Washington, D.C., and there we watch the television news. The difference between the exciting life of the city and the boring life of a small agricultural village on the open Plains becomes pretty obvious pretty quick. City news is full of murder and mayhem, dozens dead in tenement fires, riots, airplane crashes, endless traffic snarls, rapes, burglaries, assaults, traffic pileups, manifest and manifold horrors.

We are glad to get back as soon as we can to reports in our town of 352 about a three-headed calf born over by Holdrege, a soup supper sponsored by the Boelus volunteer fire department, new tires on the Baptist Church minivan, the opening of sales of Girl Scout cookies, a new sewage lift-station on Depot Street, and the possible sighting of an armadillo in Central City.

SOMETIMES BORING IS GOOD,
EVEN IN SEX

An arrangement that one sees less and less of and which receives far too little attention these days is a man and a woman—together and married. Boring stuff. A plain old marriage. I don't want to get too mushy here, but I like being married—even boringly married. I like Linda, and there are indications now and then that she actually likes me, a far less likely transaction I will freely, even gleefully admit. But one thing I can tell you, and that you have been told before, is that a very essential part of marriage is a sense of humor.

> *Marriage always demands the finest arts of insincerity possible between two human beings.*
> — VICKI BAUM,
> 1888–1960

They say most marital problems arise from finances, and I can see that. Mostly, one person in a marriage makes the money, and the other spends it. Okay, spends it on things like rent, food, clothing, transportation, and that kind of thing, but the fact of the matter is one person earns the money, or more of it, and the other spends it, or more of it. And that means trouble.

My situation is a little different because I have somehow always managed to turn my extravagances into profit. Thing is, I'm a nut. When I get interested in, say, wine, I really get interested. In fact, it becomes an obsession. I did that once with wine. I took classes, studied, worked at it, and traveled to Europe on pennies, drowned myself in wines and learned every single thing I could about wine. And people started asking me about wine, and how to make it, and I started brokering wine grapes and selling yeasts and tools and chemicals and equipment and teaching classes. The next thing I knew, I was making money with wine.

Same with folklore, and tractors, and almost everything else I've ever done in my life. Anything worth doing is worth overdoing, a buddy once told me, and I have followed that philosophy ever since. Linda learned that early on, and because she had nothing to begin with, she figured she had nothing to lose. So she let me flail around wildly, knowing that as idiotic and expensive as whatever I was doing at the moment might seem, there was a good chance that somewhere down the line it was going to pay off.

That's true of most people, but most people don't trust themselves that much, yet their spouses. And that's a shame. Riches lie in personal passion, not in logic and duty. The German philosopher Kant once drew a false dichotomy, since embraced by any number of idiots between Duty and Inclination, Pflicht und Neigung. They are, in fact, the same thing. Ultimately it is our duty to follow our inclinations and our inclination to follow our duty.

MÉNAGE À DEUX . . .
SYNERGY UP THE YIN-YANG

Perhaps the single most important notion in marriage, a considerable departure from every other arrangement and yet one that seems to be systematically ignored in modern relationships, is that you "become of one flesh." I don't think that means that a man and woman become one because of some religious doctrine; I think it's more a religious recognition of how a good marriage works, no matter what the faith of the couple. I believe that the ritual of marriage actually means that you surrender your singleness and become a part of a unit. I have nothing that isn't Linda's; she has nothing that isn't mine. Nothing.

That doesn't mean we've surrendered our uniqueness as human beings. Not by a long shot. I hope I've made that obvious already in these pages. She and I are anything but the same! Talk about two individuals!

LINDA	**ME**
Country music	Rock 'n' roll
Catholic	Non-Catholic
Sweet, gentle, soft	Loud, obnoxious, blunt
Eats off plates with silver	God gave us fingers
John Deere	Allis Chalmers
Female	Male
Czech	German
Lid up	Trees don't have lids
Steaks medium	Steaks rare
Cats	Dogs

This list could go on forever. She sleeps warm; I sleep cold. She sleeps with fan noise; I hate fan noise. We are of two different generations. Going to town to buy beans, she will buy one can; I buy a case. But just as carbon and iron combine to make steel, cold and heat meet to give us rain, and gin joins with tonic to produce headaches, Linda and I are, despite our differences, one.

I have really tried to tell my children in their marriages that you need to cave in. Not on principle, but on whatever you can do to make your other part comfortable, even happy. On a couple occasions Linda has expressed an uneasiness about something I am doing—flirting with a female friend, missing suppertime, farting—and it seems to me a small thing simply to do what I can to make little adjustments to keep her happy. After all, she's Linda.

Except for the country music thing. That's just asking too much. Country music makes my jaw tight, gives me the fantods, the collywobbles. Linda knows that. And she caves in on this one. She can't stand to see a grown man cry, unless he's wearing a hat that's way too big and whining about how nobody loves him to a country tune that sounds like every other country tune composed over the last fifty years. Then she thinks a crying man is cute.

Marriage is not a bringing together of two people of two minds but of two people who somehow speak to each other's mutual inadequacies. I don't want to be married to a great writer. That would crush me and my aspirations to be a writer. I want someone who takes care of those parts of my life where I am not. Linda is an artist; I don't know squat about art. I'm her writer; she's my artist. See how it works?

CONNUBIAL BLITZ

I purposely made the subject of sex separate from marriage because married sex isn't the same as unmarried sex. While married sex is seen as worse than unmarried sex, that's only the belief, not necessarily the truth. And remember: I'm a trained folklorist so I know about such things. Married sex is usually understood to be pretty tired and boring.

DOCTOR: Avoid any kind of excitement for a couple of months.

CARDIAC PATIENT: Will I still be able to have sex?

DOCTOR: Yes, but only with your wife.

Maybe that's the best part about married sex—no pressure. And that's something a lot of married couples miss taking advantage of. The worst part of fooling around is the constant threat of inadequacy. When you do it with your wife, you don't have to worry about that problem because your wife is already accustomed to your inadequacy.

Did that come out right? Anyway, you know what I mean.

COMMUNICATATING [*SIC*]

There is always a lot of talk about how marriage failures are caused by a lack of communication. Actually, the most common cause of divorce is marriage, but that aside, sometimes no matter how hard you try, communication simply isn't there. As I've explained before, we speak different languages. I won't tell you her name because she is a very prominent figure in politics and a good friend of ours. She told Linda and me her story in confidence, but even as she was telling it, it struck me as a remarkable example of what goes wrong in marriage.

This woman did everything she could to keep her marriage going, to make her mate happy, up to and including eating the heels of each and every loaf of bread that came through their household, the "garbage" part of any loaf of bread, as everyone knows. They didn't have a lot of cash to spare and she just couldn't bring herself to discard it like garbage. Being a good woman, with a kind heart, and loving her husband, she made the sacrifice and ate the heels herself.

At the divorce hearing, her about-to-be-former husband told the court that an example of her reckless selfishness in the union had been her insistence on eating what he and his family considered the premium part of any loaf of bread (as I do) THE HEEL! The woman's greatest sacrifice in the marriage had been interpreted by her mate as the primary example of her selfishness!

EATING IN

We laughed after she told the story, but to me it was painful. How sad, really. One of my favorite Plains writers is O. E. Rölvaag. In his first novel, he has his pioneer Norwegian family bringing forth a son, whom they arrogantly name Peder Victorious. The gods don't like that kind of pride so, no readers were surprised when, in a subsequent work, Rölvaag portrayed Peder Victorious as the very ultimate in family shame and humiliation.

What do you suppose this kid did to destroy every fiber of decency in his family's heritage? Yep, you guessed it. This Lutheran Norski married [gasp, choke] an Irish Catholic! Oh, what shameful behavior this dreadful new and savage land visited upon its peoples, huh? But the marriage was its own revenge: while this couple managed to accommodate each other's religion, there was one thing Mr. Victorious could never come to tolerate within his wretched, barbaric wife's culture. Her cooking.

There's that, too. Even when the hot excitements of sex have simmered down to a controllable comfort level, there is still that damnable dinner plate to deal with. Linda's former relationship (she won't permit me to utter his name) once ordained from his lofty superiority, "Rog will never wait for you to learn how to cook." Well, surprise, bozo-boy. About once a week I declare a meal a Michael Meal and ask Linda if I couldn't just once call this idiot and tell him about how she has indeed learned to cook. She says no, and there's not a chance in hell he'll read this, but the damn fool threw away a wonderful woman, because, in part, 1) he couldn't appreciate her ability to learn and 2) he rather naively admitted his own inability to learn.

Women can learn to cook. So can men. It's not that big a deal. For one thing, Linda came to me with a rich culinary tradition. No, not her Czech background, or her Nebraska background. The culture of the young-woman-who-left-home-and-worked-as-a-secretary-before-she-had-a-chance-to-pick-up-her-mother's-kitchen-secrets tradition. As she herself has put it, she came from a background in which every dish she cooked had one of the two words "helper" or "surprise" in it. (I once asked her why it's called "tuna surprise" and she explained that it's because I should be surprised that she bothered to cook anything at all that particular evening.)

Probably the toughest gustatorial adventures in our home are those Fridays when Linda needs comfort food, which is to say, just days before she knows I'm going to be around all weekend. Which means macaroni and cheese, always with creamed peas for reasons that escape me, other than maybe a pervading motif of bland. Or when she feels a particular spiritual need to convert me to Catholicism by feeding me salmon patties. Those evenings our marriage experiences particular strain.

Believe me, I am aware of the jeopardy I am putting myself into here, lecturing about how to make a marriage successful. This very afternoon, Laura Bush (yes, the one with two willful, booze-swilling daughters) is lecturing America on how to raise its children. Prayer in school sure didn't help those hellions, it rarely does. Kids see right through superficial and hypocritical self-righteousness and do what they can to spit in its face. Every time. So I know that I am taking something of a risk telling you here why I think our marriage is successful, but here goes anyway. . . .

SPACE CADETS

There is some general knowledge floating around saying that a woman worries about the future until she gets a husband, while a man never worries about the future until he gets a wife. Just as true, however, is the saw that a woman makes her commitment expecting he will change, but he never does; a man marries a woman assuming she will never change, and she always does.

Small wonder then that the most successful societies are those in which marriage involves unrelenting mutuality, constant accommodation, grinding constancy. I don't care how much you love each other, there simply has to be some time apart. Yes, you *are* now *one* unit, but jeez. As a dear friend of mine once said when confronted with a potential dalliance, "Yeah, sure I'm married, but I'm not a fanatic about it!"

The Vikings sailed the world, conquering lands far, far beyond the ken of other European adventurers. Why? Some say it's because Nordic women invented lutefisk, but I think it was the long, isolated polar nights that did it. I don't care how gorgeous those flaxen-haired Nordic maidens were, enough is enough.

War was invented by men to give them a chance to get out of the house. Same with hunting and fishing. Both activities are impossibly uncomfortable and expensive. So, why would men do something inherently and inevitably uncomfortable and expensive? Because it removes them from a situation that is even more uncomfortable and expensive. That's why Mormon pioneers came up with missions to far away lands. That's the point; they were far away. And why the Pawnee and Lakota went on buffalo hunts and vision quests. And why Americans commute. I've known lots of men who got and kept jobs simply to get out of the house. I know, a pretty dreadful equation.

SWINGING

Many guys have asked me about wife swapping. Well, okay, a couple guys have asked me about wife swapping. Actually, no one has asked me about wife swapping, but I keep getting the feeling that some guys would like to ask me about wife swapping. But not for my wife. I don't mean to imply that Linda wouldn't be a prime prize in the jackpot or that my pals wouldn't be interested in her. And I sure don't mean to suggest that any one of my buddies' wives wouldn't be an enjoyable morsel, or that I'm some kind of sick jealous guy, or that I am insecure about my own sexuality. I mean, hey, I've been around, and size isn't everything. And . . .

You get the idea. What people do around here when the evening gets along and romance is in the air, we've been drinking a little with a bunch of close friends . . . I mean people we've known for years and trust and feel comfortable with, just having a good time, a few drinks. People we love and trust, getting a little crazy, we throw our car keys into a pile in the middle of the table. The men close their eyes and reach out and grab a key. Whoever's car keys they get, that's the guy they get to go fishing with that weekend. That works out pretty well.

DIVORCE

I maintain that anyone who's been married only once has no sense of humor, but nothing is more destructive to a sense of humor than a marriage up in flames. I have spent a couple months now, as I have been working at this book, trying to think of something funny to say about divorce. Damned if I can think of one single thing. Even jokes about divorce are not funny—e.g., Know why divorces are so expensive? Because they're worth it. Why are you two still married? Cheaper to keep her.

> *My advice to you is get married: if you find a good wife you'll be happy; if not, you'll become a philosopher.*
> **—SOCRATES**

I don't know how many people I have watched approach divorce as rational, decent, good-hearted folks and come out of the cauldron insane with anger, filled with spite, and perfectly prepared to commit murder if they just had some assurance they could get away with it. Maybe even if they couldn't. As Marty Winch, whoever he is, once said, "It's better to be wanted for murder than not to be wanted at all."

My impression is that the angriest parties in divorces are the men, and my experience is that they have good reason for that. The process seems to be that the Poor Fragile Flower of the relationship, the one who argues elsewhere that women should enjoy precise equality with males, receives the protection of the courts and is given everything the poor sap owns except his shampoo (the opened bottles at least) and his junior high school stamp collection.

Next thing you know, this miserable joe is watching television and has to endure yet another television episode with Oprah, or Sally Jessy, or any number of other alpha bitches lamenting the universal dereliction of men who simply won't cough up their monthly tribute. "What kind of man," they ask, "won't support his own children? Tsk tsk tsk . . . what brutes these males be . . . "

Never mind that there is not a scintilla of accountability or responsibility for the woman in question to SPEND these funds on the children. I knew a woman who impoverished her former husband for child support, funds she then spent on ski trips to Aspen to find another husband while her children sold matches on street corners. Okay, it wasn't quite that bad, but the part about the ski trips is true.

I was once told by a divorced woman of my pained acquaintance that the reason there wasn't $15 in her budget to send the man's daughter to violin summer camp and yet there *was* money for a new car for her and a resodding of the lawn of the house (that used to be his, by the way) was that—and I am, no kidding, quoting here, "The most important thing for children is to have a happy mother. And that's what your money is providing your children. A happy mother."

A judge would instantly take care of a situation like that, right? I can see you've never been through a divorce.

I'm getting to be an old guy, and I've nursed some men through divorce. I have had to plead again and again for practicality, expedience, and common sense: watch your step, guard your back, don't roll over and expose your underbelly. In every single case the men have done exactly that, and in most cases (but not all, thank God) the woman in question has sanguinely, or even with visible glee, plunged the sword and twisted it, just to see the puppy scream and bleed.

Nothing funny about divorce. Nothing at all. At my last survey, murder will get you five or six years. Divorce is a poison that can go on and on and on and on . . . My advice? Take what is yours, everything that is yours, and get the hell away. Don't play games. Just get away with what you can and pray that some other fool eventually relieves you of the burden by sniffing the same cheese and stepping into the same trap.

Sauce for The Goose, Sauce for The Gander

Once again let me remind you all, dear students, that I am speaking here about general cases, the usual, the traditional, the norm, the average. I am currently involved in my capacity as the Love Doctor with the breakup of a marriage where everything is all mixed up, nothing is predictable or average or boringly conventional. In this particular case, it was the woman of the marriage who strayed. Not all that unusual, I find. But the more I learn about this particular and peculiar relationship, the more I wonder why this woman didn't dive out on this half-witted, boorish clod a lot earlier in the relationship.

He probably would have come off in the moment of quiet following the nuclear explosion as a victim, a poor guy who was done wrong, an object of sympathy and understanding. But no. This bonehead is screaming irrationally, making incredibly idiotic demands and claims, pulling underhanded and ugly financial and property gymnastics, generally being a first-class, industrial-grade asshole. And in so doing he has neatly converted himself from the victim, which he most assuredly was in the beginning, to an idiot who is getting precisely what he has coming. Nice going, stupid. This kind of foolishness makes it harder for all the rest of us men.

Easy Way Out

Inevitably, in any conversation with men who've been through the American divorce system (and probably among women, but I don't know, they don't include me in many discussions of this sort), murder arises as a possible alternative to divorce. Oh, quit acting like you're shocked! You know I'm telling nothing but the truth here. I mean jeez, as I noted before, you get six or seven years for murder, but a divorce and its consequences can drag on for decades. While in some cases a felony like this can give you some trouble down the line, in other situations I can imagine it might actually help a fellow out.

Imagine, for example, that you are dating this woman, or living with her, and you decide it isn't working. And you are trying to figure out an easy way to get out of this mess. Well, if you haven't told her before, you can sit down with her and give her a heartfelt confession of how you murdered a previous woman in your life. And then maybe chuckle when you finish up the conversation.

If this woman already knows about your past, start watching television shows on any of several cable channels that deal with murder, mayhem, crime, and scandal. Take notes, making sure she sees you doing this. If the inoculation still doesn't take, try some vigorous head nodding and muttered responses like "Yeah, that'd work!" or "Sure, but where exactly can I get that much rat poison?"

A problem does come to mind here. And again, I speak from painful experience. Linda and I were watching a news report not long ago about a woman who hired what she thought was a professional shooter to kill her husband. Well, the guy she tried to hire turned out to be a cop and she is on her way to prison.

Linda has frequently mentioned how nice it would be to be in a convent or prison where she could work quietly at her art talents without dealing with the "ugly, constant, painful, disgusting complications in her life," whatever the heck *they* might be, which means that going to prison for a couple years could be considered a win-win situation for her. So, I asked her, "Linda, you wouldn't hire someone to shoot me, would you?"

"No, dear," she replied sweetly. "I'd just send out the word for volunteers."

Just this very morning I was moving a rifle from the house out to my shop and Linda asked, "Is that thing loaded?" Now, you may have noticed that early in this book, way back in the acknowledgements,

I thanked Linda for never asking me how to *load* a gun, so you can imagine my uneasiness about her trying to find out if any items of our standard American arsenal might be *already* loaded.

I expressed my concern about her question and she laughed it off, saying, "I'd never shoot you, Rog. You know I don't like loud noises." Now, I probably should have stopped right there, but I only found further uneasiness in the clear information that the sole reason she wouldn't shoot me is because of the noise. So I asked, "Then . . . you *would* stab me?"

Again she laughed off the idea, saying, "Why would I do that? I'd just give you a couple uninterrupted days in the shop and let you bleed to death out there." Once a nurse was having a hard time pinning down a vein in my arm from which to extract blood and Linda piped up, "Just give him a butter knife and in five minutes you'll have all the blood you need."

In other words, she's going to let me kill myself. And in the case of some divorces I've seen, that would be a merciful alternative.

CHAPTER 8

THE MECHANICS OF A HOUSEHOLD

Women upset everything. When you let them into your life, you find that the woman is driving at one thing and you're driving at another.

—G. B. SHAW, *PYGMALION*

D ating is a tough process but it's *nothing* compared to sharing living quarters with a woman, especially if the condition is locked down by a marriage ceremony. Married, you are now in the situation of doing the impossible: reconciling a man and woman living together as one. That is a wonderful ideal, a dream, a hope, a prayer, a struggle, but above all an impossibility. God bless those who make it.

Perhaps a methodology for avoiding this lockdown lethargy was suggested by my own father's hint at how he and my mother survived rather comfortably living together for more than sixty-five years. Every marriage counselor, sociologist, sickologist [sic], and police officer specializing in domestic disturbances will tell you that the most common single problem ever arising in this oil/water, anchovies/chocolate cake, beer/milk, never-mix never-worry struggle of man and woman living together is money.

Linda is marvelously frugal. I think the only problem we have had in our years together was the time I went up to the tavern for an evening with my buddies, opened my billfold to buy a round and found $6 and a note saying, "This should be enough." On that occasion I laid down the law when I got home, made it clear that as the breadwinner I had my own opinion about what is "enough," and that I expected some major changes in money management in our household. So now when I go to the tavern, I sometimes find as much as $10 in my billfold.

Anyway, back to my Old Man. Mom and Dad were once regaling us with the story of their own courtship and marriage. It was during very hard times. They were very young and the only term to describe their condition was "struggle." Mom told us that was the way in old German households at the time, each week she turned her paycheck over to her foster parents and had for her own use precisely nothing. She was paid for her week's work the day before she and Dad were married, and she came to the marriage with precisely nothing. Dad had to buy her wedding dress and he borrowed the money for their marriage license.

Tears came to Mom's eyes as she remembered her pain and fear at that fateful, dramatic, youthful moment in her life. I turned to Dad and said, "Well, you weren't exactly a high roller in those days, Pop. What did you bring to the marriage?"

He thought a moment and said, "Ninety-two dollars in postal savings. On the day we were married, I turned that money over to Mom—every cent I had in this world."

Ouch. More pain and tears. "Well, Dad," I said, trying to bring some moment of cheer into this painful history lesson, "Was she worth it?"

Without hesitation he snapped back, "Time will tell, Rog. Time will tell."

They had been married over sixty-five years but, in Dad's mind everything was still tentative. I'm not sure that's a bad idea.

Dad didn't feel trapped because, hey! Everything was still on probation! He could have reclaimed his $92 and gone his merry way just about any time he wanted to. But he was still married and with Mom—because he wanted to be still married and with Mom! Not bad, huh? Instead of living together and pretending to be married, the solution may be to be married and pretending that you are living together.

I have known a lot of couples who have maintained separate bank accounts, separate property, figuring out at the end of each month who owes what. It never works. Either you're one household or you're not. Make up your mind. But you can always keep in mind: *"Time will tell."*

By way of a precaution, gents, start skimming and keep a separate and secret fund. Every time you go up to the tavern with $12, put one away. That way, when you are thrown out on your ear, you should have amassed enough to buy one more round.

MEN, REMEMBER WHO HAS THE GOODS (AND THE GOODIES)

I knew of one extreme couple who shared their monies but kept a bizarre accounting of who had brought what into the marriage and who bought what and therefore who owned what. This guy actually insisted that he should maintain control over the remote control because he had bought the television set. I once suggested that she had come to the marriage with *something* of value, if you catch my drift. He didn't catch my drift. Within weeks of the moment I heard that story the lovely lady was on her way. She had taken her goods of value and moved on to someone who would understand and appreciate such assets. But my bewildered friend had his television remote.

Frankly, I'm surprised there aren't more divorces—and murders—over remote controls. I think I have made my point fairly clear that men and women have virtually nothing in common.

Nothing. So struggle and compromise is required at every step of any effort to spend so much as an evening together. My favorite shows are:

BattleBots

Cold Cases (murder mysteries)

Real TV

COPS (especially where a dog runs down a bad guy and chews him up real good)

Hockey (or anything else dealing with war)

The Man Show

Meet the Press

Ally McBeal (babes)

Anything I'm on

Anything with W.C. Fields

Anything with explosions and car chases

Anything with even a suggestion of a naked woman

Anything with even a suggestion of a woman I would like to see naked

Anything but the Country Music Channel

On the other hand, Linda likes:

Touched by an Angel

Oprah

It's a Wonderful Life (over and over and over and over and over and over and . . .)

Friends

Providence (six minutes of this snoozer and you'll have diabetes)

Will and Grace

Ally McBeal ("cute guys")

Anything heartwarming

Awards shows no matter how trivial and arcane

Anything with Brad Pitt

Anything on the Country Music Channel

I don't care how strapped your finances are, you either need two television sets or two houses.

There are, of course, other property issues: tools, porno magazines, and cooking utensils. The first two probably won't surprise you but almost every couple I know runs into trouble when it comes to kitchen tools and appliances. Men have their favorites, women theirs: I like cast iron, big knives, and large crockery bowls; Linda has her favorite cereal bowl, her favorite soup bowl, her favorite pudding bowl, her favorite cereal spoon, favorite soup spoon, favorite pudding spoon, favorite milk glass, favorite water glass, favorite whiskey sour glass, favorite salad fork, favorite dessert fork, favorite meat fork, favorite vegetable fork, favorite . . . Well, you get the idea.

In our family we have solved these problems very tidily, I think, in that we not only have separate television sets, we have separate kitchens. They're not even in the same house. I'm not kidding. She has the kitchen in the house and I have a small outdoor summer kitchen where I can cook lutefisk, buffalo liver, barbecue ribs, corned beef hash, turtle eggs, whatever I want. Sometimes all at the same time.

WASHED UP

I have interviewed dozens of wedding planners, counselors, ministers, and anthropologists about what couples soon to be married should consider to ease their path into what will almost certainly be the most trying time of their lives (unless they are captured by savages in New Guinea, force-marched through the steaming jungle, kept in a tiny little bamboo cage, fed monkey meat and fat ants, and forced to listen to accordion music for a year). None of them so much as mentioned the laundry room. They spoke loftily of sex, money, religion, politics, and diet plans, but not a word about laundry. For all the ink spilled over the Eternal Gender Struggle ("Lid up? Lid down?"), that tension is minor compared with what goes on in every mixed gender household on a daily basis over a pile of soiled laundry.

QUADRA-D

What you can expect is what I call Quadra-D—the Double-Deal Disaster Dilemma. It may be only a Woman School variation on SNUBB, Situation Normal: Uninformed Bozo Bewildered, a tactic dealt with in an earlier chapter, but the laundry room variation is sufficiently different to deserve just a little bit of room here. Here's how it works (or perhaps more precisely, doesn't work) in our household.

MONDAY: Linda complains that I soil far too much laundry for a normal human being, thereby burdening her Monday work excessively. I express regrets and start to work at solving the problem, as the Male Human is wont to do.

TUESDAY: I set about doing my own laundry to save Linda the problem. Later in the day she notes that I have washed coloreds with whites, cottons with synthetics, dainties with shop rags, burlaps with silks, carburetor parts with dessert dishes, dogs with cats, etc. I express regrets and set myself to solving the problem, as the Male Human is wont to do.

WEDNESDAY: I forget to clean the lint trap and cause a minor house fire. I leave the dryer door open, which Linda insists wears out the little light bulb in there, which, when it burns out, takes six months for me to repair. I express regrets and set myself to solving the problem, as the Male Human is wont to do.

THURSDAY: Linda notices that I have worn the same clothes for four straight days in my effort to cut down on the amount of household laundry. She makes it clear that if I don't change at least my shirt, I will be sleeping henceforth in my summer kitchen. It's winter, and it's cold out there. I express regrets and set myself to solving the problem, as the Male Human is wont to do.

FRIDAY: Linda notices and objects to the fact that I have draped my overalls, shirts and socks over our backyard fence in an effort to avoid the lint screen and light bulb problem in the dryer. She expresses some concern about the traffic piling up on the highway as people slow down to enjoy the sight of my clothing drying in the winter wind, frozen stiff as a board. I express regrets and set myself to solving the problem, as the Male Human is wont to do.

SATURDAY: I devote a good part of the day to working in my shop, walking in the woods, and trying to resolve the contradictions of how I can wear fewer clothes and more clothes at the same time, do the laundry and yet not do the laundry, help but stay out of the way, decode the arcane hierarchy of what clothing is washed with what, and so on . . .

Have you ever looked at the choices on a washing machine and dryer? Warm, hot, cold, warm and hot, cold and cold, regular and dainty, full cycle, half cycle, double rinse, big load, medium load, small load, tap water, well water, bottled water, no press, permanent press, freedom of the press. I spend the evening watching the Discovery Channel show about sex in the Bible, *Great Explosions* on the History Channel, and *Robotica*, thinking longingly of tribes in South America that wear nothing but a strip of bark and just throw it into the campfire when it gets splintery. I make a note to check on any possible Web sites featuring disposable overalls.

SUNDAY: Somehow I forget everything that has transpired the previous week. I have no idea why.

MONDAY: Linda complains that I soil far too much laundry for a normal human being, thereby burdening her Monday work excessively. I express regrets and set myself to solving the problem, as the Male Human is wont to do.

WHEN YOU GOTTA GO, YOU GOTTA GO

A quick look at female anatomy makes it pretty clear that a unisex bathroom makes no sense at all. We bring different plumbing to the bathroom and therefore it only makes sense to offer up different plumbing when we arrive. The fact of the matter is, for most men a bathroom isn't really all that necessary. Most men I know prefer peeing on the front lawn, patio, rear tire of a pickup truck or in unison with a pack of dogs (my own personal favorite). I don't know of a single woman who takes pleasure in writing in the snow or carving out little castles in the sand with pee or trying to move a urinal cake in the manner of a hockey puck over to the drain. Nor, for that matter, do I know a woman who can. Let's face it: women are really not very good at peeing, which probably accounts for the lack of pleasure they take in the process.

Linda thinks I have carried too far my own delight in peeing in full, hot sunlight or on a crisp starry night in the company of my black Labs right there in our backyard. But to me this is far more than relieving myself of watery wastes. What I like to do is go up to the town tavern and drink a couple Heinekens with my buddies. Yes, it's good beer, but there's more to it. While I am enjoying myself, I am also performing a major international service, for all the world like Mother Teresa serving the poor of India, except I'm serving populations of two continents.

Here's the thing: where is Heineken from? That's right, Holland. And what is Holland's historic and constant struggle? That's right: fighting back the sea. That's what the dikes are all about, and the windmills—pumping water up out of the soggy bottomlands of the Netherlands, much of the nation being well below sea level. And what is the very foundation of beer? Of course, water. And what is the historic and constant struggle of America's Great American Desert, the Great Plains? You know, like Nebraska? Yep, right again: drought, no water.

I'm just one lonely man, but all great causes begin with one lonely man or woman. What am I doing? I am, bottle by bottle, taking excess water from the Netherlands and putting it well upland on the American Plains. What's even more heroic, I do what I can to hold it until I get back down here to my farm, only 500 yards from the mighty gorge of the Middle Loup River of Nebraska.

When I come home from the tavern and pee in the backyard, I am putting water on the sand that over the year regains its purity and finds its way to the raging rapids of the Middle Loup. And then that water begins its long and mystic trip down to the Platte, watering crops and fields along the way, generating electricity at power stations, providing recreation for communities all along the way. Then it empties into the muddy Missouri, where it floats barges of grain, gravel, fibers, and junked Toyotas to St. Louis and the mighty Mississippi.

Here it joins water from all across America, from the historic Appalachians to the rugged Rockies, now carrying even greater loads on its broad shoulders. Through the Deep South the deep waters course, and then finally out into the open salt waters of the Gulf of Mexico, across the Atlantic to Europe, through the Panama Canal to the Orient.

I think of all that when I at long last get home from the tavern and with my own mighty sigh of relief and appreciative smiles from my good ol' dogs, put that water on its first step, onto the sands and grass of my backyard.

No, that's okay. I understand. Linda also tells me to shut up and go to sleep, so I'm used to it.

I know what you're saying. You live in town and the neighbors are stuffy about you peeing on the lawn when they are entertaining the in-laws in their backyard just before they marry off their ugly daughter. While it might amuse the dogs even more, pooping back there amuses the Little Lady even less, especially if she's the one who mows the lawn. Okay, let me tell you what to do: Get an outhouse. There are lots of them to be found abandoned around the rural countryside and nothing is more delightful to the activist soul than pooping *in plein air.* I am working on a separate volume on outhouses, America's architecture, so I'll save a good part of this for later, but do keep in mind that that is what you need—an outhouse.

There is, clearly, more to a bathroom than the toilet. (I would, in fact, argue that the last thing that belongs in a bathroom *is* a toilet. Doesn't it bother you just a tad to sit there pooping, knowing that not two feet away is your toothbrush? Well, it bothers me.) There is, for example, the medicine cabinet, maybe a linen closet, perhaps a vanity. Before you commit yourself to sharing a bathroom with a woman, make sure you do visit her in her native lair and make some excuse about needing to go to her bathroom, something subtle about not feeling comfortable peeing on *her* front lawn, or off her seventh-floor balcony. Although you'll have to admit that sounds like an awful lot of fun, it might be wise to save that adventure for later in your relationship.

Once you have gained entry to her most private of privacies, lock the door and spend some time looking around. Prepare yourself to be amazed. For one thing, there are little bitty bars of soap with flowers on them at the sink that have never been used. Those really are bars of soap but you're not supposed to wash your hands with them or anything else either. Soap, this most functional of items, is decorative in a woman's bathroom, and you're going to be in real trouble if you use the ones with flowers on them. Same with the little towels and washcloths with the pretty embroidery. Want to get out of a relationship? Wash your hands with the little soaps and dry them on the embroidered towels.

Look in the linen cupboard or vanity. (Not the medicine chest. Not yet. That requires a special introduction. You could really hurt your psyche looking into a woman's medicine cabinet without emotional preparation.) Don't touch anything; she knows exactly where it is and would sense your prying in a second. Just look in wonder. A special post-shampoo, pre-conditioner rinse for semi-oily hair with split ends and sun-induced "blossoming," whatever the hell that is. You had no idea she had semi-oily hair, and if you have any brains at all, you won't mention it. About the most you can say about a woman's hair is that it is pretty and smells good.

Open the medicine cabinet only if you are a strong man and are really, seriously considering this woman for a mate. If the mediations and ministrations for her hair weren't complicated and disturbing enough, wait until you open up that medicine chest! There are cures there for medical problems you had no idea existed, and for conditions that you didn't think were problems. Kneecap fungus? What the hell is kneecap fungus? Does she have it or is she only, hopefully, keeping this stuff on hand for a female friend who stays over occasionally? Can you catch it? How would you know?

Navel-ring lubricant? Bag balm? Lip-gloss undercoat primer? Eyebrow plucking unguent? Underarm after-shave irritant balm? Mace?

If there was ever a case for don't ask, don't tell, this is it. Thing is, if you team up with this woman, that stuff is going to be in your bathroom medicine chest—or more precisely, what used to be your bathroom medicine chest. My advice stands: get yourself an outhouse, a tin basin, and a bucket. Put a shelf in the privy to hold your deodorant, razor, toothbrush, and curry comb. Abandon what was once yours. Declare it a male-free zone. Believe me, my friend, you don't want to go back in there again.

While you are in your new lady friend's bathroom, take a look at her reading material. Sit down for ten minutes, even if you don't need to. Read one of her magazines. Is that dreadful, or what? Etch into your brain: another reason Rog is right; this is not a bathroom I want to spend time in.

A couple months ago my buddy, Woodrow, came stumbling into my study and said he needed a couple minutes to talk with me privately. From the utterly stupefied look on his face, I could tell he was serious.

Woodrow is a plumber. And he had just been to a plumbing convention. And he had picked up a videotape, and he really needed some help. I popped the video into the VCR and understood at once his confusion. He has been a plumber all his life, and here he was, looking at a video outlining how to install a bidet, or as he pronounced it, bite-it. He explained that he understood perfectly well how to install this thing, but he could not for all the world, understand what the hell it was for.

> *Home life as we understand it is no more natural to us than a cage is natural to a cockatoo.*
> —G. B. SHAW,
> *GETTING MARRIED*

I looked at Woodrow and thought about how to deal with this bit of his education. Bidets are not your standard bathroom appliance in America, right? Imagine for a moment how many bidets there might be within a 500-mile radius of where I'm sitting right now, smack in the middle of Nebraska, smack in the middle of America.

My first acquaintance with a bidet was a sort of mixed-emotions event. I was staying with some really great folks in Paris, and they knew how to treat a very young, very provincial lad right. They were like a team of trained ethnologists, showing me the very best, and the very worst of Paris, but finest of all, the most typical. I can't remember how long I was there, probably a week or two but it seemed like years.

The man of this family went off to work long before I was up. I would drag out of bed about 10:00 A.M., wander downstairs where the housekeeper had some wonderful coffee, some croissants, a fine jelly, and some fruit waiting on the table. Then I would go out and walk the streets for a few hours. A DuBonnet at a café on the Champs-Elysées, watching flics beat up Algerian troublemakers or observing car accidents. (At the time the Champs was eight lanes of traffic wide, but without lane markers. This transformed ordinary city traffic into a wonderful spectator sport that makes today's NASCAR drivers look like girlie-boys.) Mid-afternoon I would buy an incredible baguette and wander back to the house. My friend and his wife returned about 5:00 or 6:00 for mixed drinks. We sat and drank while the housekeeper-cook drove us crazy with kitchen aromas.

Then an evening meal like I had never imagined. It would begin about 8:00 or 9:00, and came drifting to the table one dish at a time with lots of time between deliveries. It was the first time in my life I hadn't just gulped a supper as if it were a kind of perfunctory pit stop to be done without delay and an immediate return to the race. Then dessert, and coffee; fine dark coffee, not the pallid watery stuff of my homeland. Some dessert wine, relax-ation, time to let the meal settle, and then time to go out for the evening just about the time back home I'd have already slept for two or three hours.

One evening we broke the rhythm and for supper went out about 10:00 in the evening to a little boite called La Grenouille (The Frog). The cook there specialized in frog legs. You entered through the kitchen, where you admired the cooking, left your order, and, if you made no fuss while the cooks groped and fondled the woman with you, they gave you a little metal frog by way of a courtesy and acknowledgement. It was all very civilized.

There were maybe twenty bare wooden tables and plain benches in the dining area And maybe one hundred riotously drunk Frenchmen intent on eating more butter-and-garlic-soaked frog legs and drinking more wine and groping and fondling more women. A couple vignettes I remember with special glee: A wild man came running full tilt into the room carrying a police-man's distinctive hat, diving over a table, and without explanation sitting at a table and striking up a casual conversation. Moments later a hatless cop came roaring into the room cursing and waving a nightstick, but unable to identify the thief in the smoky, dark, crowded room. No one, it seems, had seen a thing, and conversation continued without so much as a hiccup. The cop left in a total fury. As the door slammed, the crowd erupted in a spontaneous cheer, and the man with the policeman's hat was celebrated the rest of the evening as a hero.

The second memory of the evening was the entrance of an elderly, very well-dressed man with an absolutely luscious young woman on his arm, in a dazzling dress and coat, and a plunging neckline that brought the room to a quiet buzz. We all watched this couple in wonder as they sat on opposite sides of one of the communal tables.

The waiter approached, stood behind the woman, and handed each of the newcomers a menu. They lifted the menus and began to read. The waiter casually dropped his hand down the front of the young lady's dress and for a good five minutes, while the old man fussed about how he wanted his frog legs and wine, explored every inch of that woman's breasts as if giving the rest of us a lesson in exactly how such things should be done. The woman was absolutely glowing by the time the old man dropped his menu and the waiter, smiling, took her order.

That's the kind of evening it was. Lots of butter, garlic, frog legs, hilarity, wine. My friends had an absolutely miniscule car. It was essentially a two-seater but there was a kind of luggage platform where a backseat would be in a regular automobile, so my former wife and I sat there. They had to roll back the canvas roof so I would fit in, so we drove home through the Paris night, my face and upper torso in the wind. I was twenty-two years old, dead drunk, deliriously happy, at that moment in a perfect paradise.

We all know what comes of paradises. A couple hours later I learned something of the folly of butter, garlic, hilarity, and way, way too much wine. I staggered biliously toward the bathroom to rid myself of demons. There it was—the first stop and therefore the most logical one for me and my condition—the bidet. All of which is to say, my first embracing of a bidet was in the dubious situation of being sick beyond anything anyone ever experienced during the Black Death, but at the same time perfectly dazzled that here I was, puking up superb Claret, and the finest frog legs in the world, in Paris, into a bidet. As you can imagine, bidets carry a curious double charm for me.

If your new girlfriend has a bidet, you'll probably have to put one into your bathroom too. Some day you may be grateful.

Now I Lay Me

Now that a woman is living under the same roof with you, you no longer own a bedroom. It's hers. When Linda came to my very comfortable bachelor digs, I was doing quite well sleeping on a sheet of two-inch plywood sitting atop two three-foot piles of surplus ammo boxes, with more ammo boxes set on end as bedside tables. (The theory was that the higher you are in a room, the warmer it is, and also since it was a smallish house, putting the bed three or four feet up off the floor left the entire space under the bed for storing things like suitcases, life jackets, fishing equipment, and dirty dishes.)

It was only a matter of weeks before my wonderful canvas sheets were replaced by flowery things with fitted corners and lacy frills around the edge. The plywood was out in the shed and a new bed with box springs and orthopedic mattress was installed. We had cute little bedside stands with lamps featuring Bavarian ceramic angels blowing trumpets and playing harps, and my extensive and expensive decorating scheme (centerfolds stapled onto the walls and ceiling) had been replaced with wallpaper and muted pastel paint.

I know what you're thinking: what kind of man am I to put up with that sort of abuse of my own property, by someone who has been there for only weeks? Well, fellows, something else was now in that bedroom, if you catch my drift. Frankly, economy and male-oriented decorative schemes no longer seemed of much importance to me. Still don't. As far as I'm concerned, she can do anything she wants with that room of the house as long as the welcome mat is out for me now and again.

YARD AND GARDEN

There are two sides to this next delicate consideration. You want to maintain whatever control of this part of your life as you possibly can, but you do not want to suggest that the yard and garden are your exclusive realm, because then you're going to wind up spending most of your life mowing, raking, digging, trimming, pruning, fertilizing, pest pursuing, fencing, and then more digging and mowing.

Some men really like this kind of thing. One friend of mine argues that the scream of a chain saw or roar of an unmuffled mower is a pleasant relief from his wife's urging that he get his dead butt off the couch and away from the television, get out there and take care of that lawn and garden.

In this regard I am not typical. I grew up helping my dad work on rich folks' lawns and gardens. As a result, I absolutely loathe lawns and gardens. I made it very clear to my Lovely Linda very early in our courtship that there is no way in billy-hell I intend ever again in my life to spend time mowing or raking a lawn. That, I explained, is why I have a farm and live in the country. If anyone has an argument with my system of lawn and garden care, he can talk it over with my lawn man, who is God. We are both content with that arrangement. God and me, that is—not Linda.

This has not been an easy issue in our marriage, to be sure. Linda wants a barefoot lawn, which ours sort of is if you don't mind walking on cactus, cockleburs, poison ivy, scrap metal, and puncture vine. I have given her free rein to do what she wants. I don't even argue about whatever money she spends trying to grow bluegrass and discourage cockleburs in the 99% sand we call soil, which will never grow bluegrass but is like heaven to cockleburs.

I also bought her a big, fancy riding lawn mower, with lights so she can mow at night and not embarrass me by revealing to the neighbors that she does all the lawn work around here.

WHEN SHE'S GONE, SHE'S STILL NOT GONE

The most important thing for you to do when The Woman leaves you alone at home is to make it clear that you simply cannot survive without her. Yes, I know, of course, that you can. In fact, you can prosper without her. You did just fine without her for all those years and didn't exactly die of neglect. Okay, so you had to throw away your sheets after a month or two without changing them, and there is still evidence of some things you cooked years ago on your cookware. Nonetheless, you didn't die! My bet is that you gained weight eating out of cans, you saved electricity sleeping with the dogs, you can always replace the cookware, and everyone blows sound system speakers now and then.

Take it from me, your woman is not going to understand this kind of logic. If you ever want her to leave you alone in the house again, you are going to have to do something to prepare for her I-shall-return wade ashore.

For one thing, do whatever is necessary to pin down the date of her return and make it absolutely impossible for her to return early. Buy nonchangeable airline tickets. Set things up so you can't possibly pick her up any other day but the one you have established. Call her hotel, pretend you are a police officer, and ask that they hold her overnight for observation. Whatever else happens, you must know the day she is returning from her trip.

You have to set aside your last day in paradise as mop-up day. If you have a buddy with a backhoe or power washer, make arrangements for him to be there early the morning of your last day of freedom. Hire a painter. Wear a long-sleeved shirt to cover up any visible wounds. Buy new long-sleeved shirts in case the fire in the bedroom destroyed all that you had before she left. Then work like a damn dog to return those living quarters to something close to what they were before.

BUT . . . !

But don't do it too well. I cannot stress this enough. While it is crucial that you do whatever it takes, pay whatever is required to get that place back into prime condition, you must leave at least one or two things undone! You won't learn anything more important in Man School than those ten words.

My buddy, Woodrow, leaves several cupboard doors open in the kitchen. That's enough. I leave a spoon and a cup in the sink. I wouldn't go as far as a deer carcass in the shower stall or anything like that. Maybe a beer can beside the couch, a sock on the stairs. She wants to know that you can't survive without her, and even something as small as that lonely sock on the stairs is sufficient to verify her convictions. And for Pete's sake, don't argue when she tells you what a helpless, hopeless boob you are and how you would probably be buried in garbage if she were gone longer than a week. This is a very delicate moment for you: you don't want her to think you or the house are really in danger, but she also needs to believe that when she leaves you are constantly flailing about wondering what on earth you are going to do about the garbage if she isn't there to tell you to take it out.

This theory of indispensability has two sides to it. Just as you need to convince the woman in your life that you cannot survive without her, you need to convince her that she cannot survive without you. That's not so easy, since she starts from the Woman School premise that men, have no particular or discernible function other than opening jars.

First, make a list of things she absolutely needs you for: taking dead mice out of traps, changing faucet washers, installing furnace filters, opening jars, unplugging toilets, shooting marauding bears, or checking the oil in her car.

Then make damn sure you never teach her how to do these things, or give her equipment that will, or introduce her to any other men who can do the same things. I can imagine that it would be okay to introduce your woman to a buddy who can open jars but not one who is also a plumber, for example. Keep yourself indispensable.

Whenever possible, offer misinformation about such processes. Show her a gun-cleaning rod and tell her that if she ever needs to change the furnace filter on her own, she should remember where this is hanging in the closet. Then put it out in the garage where she'll never find it. Tell her to remind you sometime when you are under the car to show her where the framgutor is that she needs for adjusting the garbage disposal the first of every month. I have gone so far as to buy Linda a piston ring compressor and give it to her, explaining that she will eventually need it to drain the septic tank if I'm not around. Think "layers of confusion."

You can even make some things up. Once a month or so crawl under the trailer or the car or the bed or the furnace or the dog and explain that it's time to realign the fargel, replace the blanjet valve, tighten the prinstel, clean the bergamot, that kind of thing. An hour or so later come crawling out, express utter exhaustion, say something like "Thank God that needs to be done only once a month. I can't believe that you'd never done that until I came along. Sometime when you feel like getting really dirty, get over your fear of snakes and spiders, and have a cold so you don't have to put up with the hideous smell, you can crawl under there with me and I'll show you how to do it for yourself in case I die or get thrown out of the house or something."

CHAPTER 9

THE YEAR—
MALE AND
FEMALE

*When two people are under the influence of the most violent,
most insane, most delusive, and most transient of passions,
they are required to swear that they will remain in that excited,
abnormal, and exhausting condition continuously until death
do them part.*

—G. B. SHAW, *GETTING MARRIED*

Not long ago I conducted a limited survey among male acquaintances and found that they had suspected the same thing I stumbled on years ago: that women systematically manipulate the calendar so that we men are constantly facing yet another circumstance requiring us to buy presents for the women in our lives. Let's just do a quick review of the year in my own household.

January

The year starts, of course, with the buying of Christmas presents. Okay, it's easy for you, and Linda, to say I should have thought of that long ago and bought Christmas presents in, say, November. But I didn't. So I am buying Christmas presents in January, and facing the tired old joke about whether I am buying late for last year or early for the next. This means, of course, I have to spend about three times more than I would with more timely purchases but that's the way men are supposed to do it, and that's the way I do it.

Linda often expects me to make sacrifices to our relationship as a part of my New Year's resolutions, like to shave daily, or twice daily, to talk nice and quiet, to fix things around the house rather than tinkering with battered old tractors out in my shop, to put up calendars featuring black Lab retrievers rather than Carmen Electra—that kind of thing. I believe in keeping promises like New Year's resolutions, even though they are made only to myself, so each and every year I make one resolution and only one resolution: I promise that in the coming year I will not eat cold, lumpy gravy. And I don't.

February

This is the month of the accursed St. Valentine's Day. Legend has it that Valentine Rudolfo once ran a candy factory in Parmesan, Italy. Business was slow and so he invented a holiday that would require every man in the world to buy candy and flowers (his brother-in-law, Florio, ran a flower shop). He was martyred when the males of northern Italy stormed his shop and drowned him in a chocolate vat. Later that same year the women in northern Italy filled out the necessary forms and nominated him for sainthood, a gesture eventually approved and sanctified by the Vatican's Women's Auxiliary.

I don't have much to offer by way of suggestions for late delivery of Christmas presents, other than buy big and often, but I have plenty of advice for you about Valentine's Day. The 24 hours of St. Valentine's Day are probably the most crucial and critical annual observation for any marriage, with the possible exception of your wedding anniversary, and whatever you do, if you've been married before, don't get those dates confused. In forty-six states confusing wedding anniversaries is accepted as a reasonable cause for homicide. Most men who make this mistake just go ahead and commit suicide on the spot. Valentine's Day is a cruel and angry time, masquerading as a romantic interlude but fraught with danger. As I write this, there is a Canadian poll saying that what most men want for this holiday is a warm, affectionate, loving evening. Thing is, the poll doesn't say who with.

At any rate, our problem is not what men might want for this day, but what women demand. Linda and I have taken two approaches to this annual crisis: 1) Hers, and 2) Mine. I will deal with hers later, under March Madness. Buying expensive chocolates, which always seems perfectly reasonable to a male and worth the price during courtship, becomes less meaningful for him as time goes along, which is to say, about fifteen minutes after the wedding reception.

I've tried to keep our household on an even keel by buying Linda chocolates for Valentine's Day—Kit Kat bars, Snickers, even Reese's Peanut Butter Cups. But my efforts have always fallen short, which was explained to me each and every year in some detail. So, in winter 2001, I decided to do things right for a change. I went out to the shop. I put my mind to work, I did some designing and calculating, I organized some materials, and I welded up a big, iron Valentine's Day heart for Linda.

This baby is an industrial-grade Valentine's Day heart. I used 3/16-inch steel, and I wasn't at all stingy with the welding rod. The final product measures about 16 x 16 inches, 3 inches deep, not counting the 24-inch iron rod I used for the arrow jauntily piercing the heart. I'd estimate that the entire package weighs in at something a touch above twenty-four pounds. I drove over it a couple times with a tractor just to show my buddies in town that this time I had really gone all out to endear myself with the missus. Not a scratch—either to me, that iron Valentine's Day heart, or the tractor.

My pals didn't know the half of it. That was just the box. It has a removable lid, also solid 3/16-inch steel, and with our initials cut through it with my plasma cutter! Next I went to Kerry's Grocery and bought a wide sampling from his jerky selection, famous throughout this area for its variety and quality. I'm not talking homemade jerky here. I'm talking store-bought, commercial, USDA-approved jerky. Almost twenty bucks worth. And I packed that iron heart with this fancy and expensive stuff.

As they say on the television commercials for magic mustache cleaning formula or a plastic radish trimmer, "But wait! There's more!" Under all that store-bought jerky I put a note: "Dear Sweetums: This is your bottomless jerky love heart! Next year I'll fill it up again for you with an extra-heavy dose of the teriyaki carp jerky! You name it, you got it!"

So, Linda was real happy, don't you suppose? She realized right off all the work and thought I'd put into this gift and she showered me with love and affection and told me I could take her birthday, our anniversary, and Mother's Day off, right?

Yeah, right, sure. She told me to get that rusty thing off the kitchen table. At this very moment it rests in a dark and cobwebbed corner of my shop storage area. So much for romance.

I am writing these words just days before another Valentine's Day. I think there are six or seven a year. As it turns out, I am going to be working out of town on February 14. This morning I found a working copy of an entry form issued by a local television station for a contest they are running, "What We Are Doing Romantic for Valentine's Day." Here's what Linda had written:

> *True to form, my favorite husband of 21 years, Roger Welsch, scheduled himself to appear at a tractor show in Kentucky on Valentine's Day! This mistake on his part has been wonderful for me because, realizing he committed a major breach of romantic etiquette, he has been the*

absolute model husband for the last two weeks. With any luck at all, I can squeeze this contrite behavior out all the way to the end of February!

I think I'm in trouble again and all the fine, gourmet jerky I bought for that iron heart isn't going to do me a bit of good. If this isn't Woman School in action, then I don't know what kind of proof it is going to take.

March, April

What's in March that requires presents, you're asking? Shouldn't St. Patrick's Day and a six-pack of green beer and orange Cheetos be enough to satisfy any Celtic lusts? Well, no. Linda's birthday is in March. So, once again I am faced with the task of buying expensive presents, cards, and romantical baubles, you're thinking, right?

Bigamy is having one wife too many. Monogamy is the same.

—OSCAR WILDE

Well, no. But this time I am not going to burden you with my whining and complaining. This is where Linda begins to shine, calenderally speaking. Linda is one smart cookie. She is smarter than most women I have met in my entire life. I have asked her specifically about her strategies for her birthday, and for the inevitable April gift opportunity, our anniversary. She was frank and honest in her response, which I quote here verbatim:

> *Rog, I realized early on that these annual observations are about as important to me as they are forgettable to you, so I knew that if I wanted to be treated the way I deserve on these special occasions, I was going to have to take things in my own hands and, as usual, take care of the little details.*

The first time she said that it made me a little nervous. When I heard "little details," Lorena Bobbitt somehow came to mind. Then I saw Linda's Woman School training kick in, and I realized why she had graduated magna cum loud from that fine center of learning.

The next day she came home from town with a very expensive, very frilly, very fancy Valentine's Day card—a red velvet heart, lots of flowers, and incredibly gooey sentiments about love, devotion, and eternity. But not a single mention, I noted, of bullets in the laundry dryer or fish bait in the fridge. Guess love, devotion, and eternity don't go that far, even on Valentine's Day. She also came home with a big, red, heart-shaped box of expensive chocolates and some silk roses.

Now, you can imagine how the cash register tapes were whirling in my head as I saw all these luxurious and pricey love tokens being unpacked. Then Linda sat me down, looked me straight in the eye, and explained how this was going to work. She said that I should read the card, do what I could to grasp its sentiments, and then sign it. I should put the card on the heart-shaped box of chocolates, lay the flowers across the top, and put it on her chair in the living room, where she would be surprised and delighted to find it later that very same evening.

Being of a romantical bent of mind, I followed orders. Later that same evening she was surprised and delighted and even kissed me on the forehead, calling me a darling. She explained that she would read the card, eat the chocolates, and sniff the flowers—and then put them away until the next February—whereupon she would get them out again. I was then to initial the card, put it on the box (which she would have refilled with good chocolates instead of the cream-filled junk you get in cheap Valentine boxes), place the silk roses on the top, and put it on her chair in the living room, where she would be surprised and delighted to find it later that evening the next year. And the next, and the next, and the next.

Which I did. And which I have done annually for the last 20 years.

Sometimes when I initial that good old Valentine's Day card I let my romantical self take over and I add comments like "Hey, kid, nice year! Let's keep it up!" or "Thanks for letting me go to Greenland!" or "You could use a little improvement on the lawn work but mostly you've been super again this year." The main thing is, I don't forget Valentine's Day or her birthday, for which she performed the same precaution, because I don't have to *remember* Valentine's Day or her birthday. She takes care of the "little details," I deal with the romanticles.

May

May is Mother's Day—another set of presents, more gooey cards, more flowers, another dinner out, pressure to plod into a movie without explosions, car chases, or gratuitous nudity. Our usual approach for this "holiday" (read: commercial rip-off) is that I negotiate a trade-off for . . .

June

Father's Day. A very bright guy once told me that the secret to his long and happy marriage was that he and his wife went out dancing twice a week. He went on Tuesdays, she went on Thursdays. That's what Linda and I do in May and June. I give her twenty bucks to go to a conversational movie in May, as long as she brings me buttered popcorn when she comes back, and I'll spend a day in the shop with a promise to hose down before she gets back. And then in June she goes to a conversational movie, as long as she brings me buttered popcorn when she comes back, and I spend the day in the shop with the promise to hose down before she gets back.

July

July is actually my celebration, although I think it should be Linda's. This is the one month I would be glad to buy big and gooey. July 4 is the day I celebrate the victory of freedom and justice over tyranny and despotism, the day when the oppressed arose and threw off their chains, a triumph of blood, sweat, and tears over the powers of the plutocracy and exploitation, a fateful moment in world history when truth triumphed and the sun rose over a new, liberated world with a future stretching out before it that would forever lighten the hearts of men.

Okay, you guessed it. It's the anniversary of the day my divorce from my first marriage became final.

As I annually point out to Linda, if it weren't for the whole miserable, unnecessary, ugly set of circumstances that led up to that divorce, the worst moments and years of my life, she and I wouldn't have wound up as life partners. Curiously, for reasons I've never quite understood, instead of going to drink, eat, and dance to celebrate my liberation and reentry into the arena of courtship, she elects every year to go down by the bridge and stare into the murky depths of the river and cry.

August

This is a big month for me because I get to go off to the reservation and celebrate the annual Omaha tribal powwow with my friends and family—good food, good music, good dance, good fun. For reasons I'll never understand, Linda is still down at the river, crying, staring into the murky depths of the river. I bring her a present.

September

Linda is a Catholic. I am not. And she says that the most sacred holiday of the Catholic calendar is Saint Godiva's Day, when men married to Catholic girls back in the Old Country pick up their heart's loves and parade them around town on their green tractors and buy them very expensive Godiva chocolates, which is why they are called Godiva chocolates.

How would I know? I never studied theology. I don't know what they believe in and what they do in the Catholic Church. I buy her the chocolates.

October

According to Linda, October is the month in the Catholic calendar for Saint Kolachy's Day. Yep, Saint Kolachy's Day, the day in October when the Vatican requires all men married to Catholic girls to watch an Oprah special with Dr. Phil mooning over troubled relationships, take them out to a salad bar for something healthy and wholesome to eat, and then take in a movie about how angels swoop down to save a woman with a difficult relationship by teaching the clodhopper sensitivity and understanding. The ending is always heartwarming. In the movie.

November

November is my birthday month, and Linda always does two things for me that are extra special and which I look forward to all the other eleven months of the year: one, she doesn't make me buy her anything this month, and two, she doesn't buy me anything this month. Okay, there is a third item, but that's none of your business.

December

This is, of course, the season of Christmas, Hanukkah, and that other most important of papal observances, St. Linda's Eve (Linda tells me), all of which require me to buy presents for Linda.

Sprinkle this yearly calendar generously with Antonia's birthday, and Mom's birthday, our anniversary, Assumption of the Blessed Gift Bearer, Linda's baptism day, Linda's confirmation day, Linda's first training bra day, the day we first met, the day we first kissed, the day we had our first argument, the day . . . well, you get the idea. At any point in the year I am rarely more than a week or two away from needing to purchase a present for some woman in my life. They plan it this way. In Woman School.

THE CALENDAR MALE

Men don't think like this. In fact, men pretty much hate seeing things like birthdays and Father's Day come around, because it only means that they are going to lose another twenty dollars, or fifty dollars, from their billfolds and receive heated socks that use forty dollars worth of batteries an hour. Or maybe a flex-shaft screwdriver with a light bulb on the end, for which you will never find a single application.

In fact, men are generally and genuinely oblivious to the cycles of the year. A friend of mine mentioned not long ago that her five children were all born in July. I did some fancy back-counting and said that I couldn't help but wonder what sort of passion must flood over her in October. Nothing of the sort, she said. October, she explained, is when deer season begins and the Old Man heads off into the woods to eat raw meat and smell bad. Every hunting season as he left, he would say, "Honey, let me give ya a little something to think about while I'm gone" and, as she said with a stern frown, "Boy, did he." The operative phrase then follows: "Whereupon he left."

Men see the year as a sequence of seasons: deer season, football season, *Sports Illustrated* swimsuit season, ice fishing season, hockey season, gin-and-tonic season. But when was the last time you bought a birthday present for a buddy other than a couple beers up at the tavern? You know as well as I do what would happen if you showed up at the duck blind with a nicely wrapped scented candle or minty herbal sachet for your hunting pal's pickup truck by way of observing formally the sixth anniversary of the first time you two went hunting together.

Men do give presents. In the past few weeks alone I got a plastic baggie of venison jerky my pal, Woodrow, had with him but hadn't finished yet. My buddy, Gene, gave me two boxes of .410 shells with #4 shot that I haven't been able to find around here.

When a man *does* give another man a gift, it is more than likely a *man* present—camping equipment, disgusting food, weapons, a dog, something like that. For example, for Christmas I gave my good friend Dave a remote-control wireless Whoopee Cushion. They are incredible—five different farting sounds and you can trigger the blasts from as far away as fifty feet. A miracle of modern technology.) I gave my son Chris a set of pipe wrenches. A son-in-law got a jerky dehydrator.

Linda gave me shaving lotion, scented soaps, extra-long-lasting deodorant sticks, a shampoo sampler, a mustache trimmer, and a case of industrial grade Beano.

Women see the year as a progression of reasons men should buy them gifts. As with Christmas, however, I make a point of *not* giving Linda gifts *on* the expected date. Even if I know her birthday is Tuesday, or Mother's Day is Sunday, or that the anniversary of the first time we ever went to a movie in Grand Island in the afternoon is Wednesday, I come to her with expensive offerings to lay at the altar of my love for her on Monday. Or Tuesday, or Thursday. Or Friday.

Before, after—it makes no difference. The thing is, while there are some small gestures of approval awaiting me if I bring my sacrifices on the very day they are expected, there is also something of a trap in leading her to expect presents *always* to appear on the day they are expected. With my deferred or anticipatory presentations system, all she knows is that sometime within a week or so of any particular gifting requirement, I will almost certainly show up with something. And I do. And she is always grateful.

A PRACTICAL GIFT GUIDE

I'm sure that if you have had any experience at all with women, and absolutely if you've had as much experience with them as I have, you know that a gift is not a gift is not a gift is not a gift.

Chocolates, flowers, diamonds, and Porsches always strike a positive chord, I have found. At least the chocolates and flowers. I've only been told about the diamonds and Porsches. No, that's not exactly it either: I have seen it in movies. But whatever the case, even flowers and chocolates have their downside: "Oh, I love chocolates. I've been trying to lose weight, and this will really throw me off." So chocolates are interpreted as often as not as your effort to subvert her best intentions.

Cut flowers fade so quickly, and it seems such a shame to cut them from the stems. Potted plants are such a problem to take care of, so they won't work either. I've told you what happened with my best efforts at welding up an iron Valentine's Day heart stuffed with prime commercial jerky. (And if that won't work, what the heck will?)

Gift certificates? I tried that. I blew a hundred bucks on a gift certificate for Linda to spend a day lounging in a spa, her every beauty requirement being met: a massage, manicure, pedicure, mud bath, hair twist, cucumber wallow, lip waxing, and a lot more things I can't even spell. She didn't like it. She said if I ever get her anything again that involves a stranger tinkering with her toes, it'll all be over. So much for good intentions.

GIFTS TO AVOID

I have taken a survey among my pals up at the tavern and here is their list of absolute no-nos when it comes to presents for the woman in your life:

- Shotgun (I actually did once buy Linda a shotgun and I can verify that if you want to indulge in an exercise in ingratitude, this is a good way to kick things off.)
- Sander (Same as above but not quite so violent a response, so you may want to keep in mind that she isn't going to be able to hurt you nearly as bad with a sander as a shotgun.)

- Ab Roller, bathroom scales, diet books, membership in any weight loss program, cases of Slimfast (Even if it's the chocolate kind.)
- Breast implants
- Cooking supplies
- Sky diving lessons
- Insurance policy (Unless it's on you, in which case you may want to give this some extra thought.)
- Season pass to the World Wrestling Federation
- Membership in the Lager-of-the-Month-Club
- Subscription to *Big Boob Babes* magazine
- A homemade booklet of coupons featuring one hour of free access to your body

GIFTS SHE'LL LIKE

After giving this chapter some considerable thought, I cannot for the life of me think of anything she'll like. I spent almost $600 on Linda this past Christmas. A lot of that went for a video camera she has been wanting for years. It's still in the box. It turns out that while she thought it would neat to have a video camera, she isn't all that crazy about actually shooting video with it.

A couple weeks after Christmas, my friend Paul Jensen sent me a gag package of goofy stuff from his printing operation: some notepads, things-to-do list pads, a bunch of sample ballpoint pens, stuff like that. Linda loved it. She had more fun with that package than all the other stuff I'd invested in for Christmas. I know, I know, we already have notepads, steno tablets, and boxes of ballpoint pens. But she liked the ones Paul sent, I guess.

She was very polite about the gifts I gave her. She was gracious and sweetly thankful. But she then said that if it was okay with me, she was going to take some of the money she'd gotten for Christmas from my mother and her parents and buy some things she really wanted for Christmas but hadn't gotten.

It's a good thing she did, because I'd never have guessed what her heart's desires were. She got a dozen coupons for full washes and hot waxes at the car wash and she bought a small utility stepladder—a plain ol' three-step ladder. I would have shopped a long time before I would have struck on the brilliant ideas of car wash coupons and a stepladder.

The bottom line is that when it comes to buying presents for women, nothing works. There is no perfect gift, maybe not even such a thing as an acceptable gift. I am going to keep at my research on this problem, and I'll get back to you when I figure something out. I'd just give her money and let her buy whatever she wants, but I'm told that's being inconsiderate.

I have struck on one thing that seems to meet with at least initial approval, if followed inevitably by disappointment: Every once in a while, sometimes on the special day requiring a gift, sometimes not, I simply revert to courtship behavior. I shower with good soap (as opposed to my favorite, Grandpa's Pine Tar Soap), shampoo with herbal something or another, splash on a little spicy after-shave, comb my hair, dress in a nice white shirt and new overalls, wear shoes (at least until supper is over), and here's the big gesture and by far and away the one that is most painful for me: give her 100% control of the remote control for the entire evening.

Linda says that's better than diamonds. It's sure cheaper than diamonds, but assuming for the short term an identity which is not at all your own is not without its hazards. I am reminded of a story often heard around my little town of Dannebrog, Nebraska, about the guy who is walking down the main street of town one Saturday evening, showing off on his arm just about the most gorgeous woman this town had ever seen. I mean, this woman was an absolute knockout. The next day, this guy's best friend waved him down and asked him, "Man, how did you ever get yourself a woman like that? What's your secret anyway?"

The friend said, "Buddy, believe me, you can get one just like that for yourself too. All you need to do is start to shave every morning, get out of those overalls and into a nice suit and tie, get a haircut, sprinkle on a little foo-foo water and before long, you will have a lady just as fancy as mine."

The guy figured it was at least worth a try. He got himself a haircut, shaved every day, put away the overalls, donned a suit and tie, and sprinkled on a generous quantity of foo-foo water. Sure enough, it wasn't a month before this guy too had a woman just as stunning as his buddy's.

He was showing *her* off, walking her down the main street of town, when out of nowhere—zap!—here comes a bolt of lightning, knocks him dead right on the spot. As you can imagine, the first thing this guy does when he gets to heaven is to look up God, and he says pitifully, "Why me? Why now?" God shakes his head, shrugs apologetically, and says, "Didn't recognize you."

I don't want to find myself in a situation like that, thank you very much.

CHAPTER 10

A GUIDE TO
FEMALE
PHYSIOLOGY

The nakedness of woman is the work of God.

—WILLIAM BLAKE, *PROVERBS OF HELL*

Y ou may have noticed somewhere along the line that
female and male human bodies are not the same. They
have insies where we have outsies. They are outsy where
we are not so outsy.

They are soft in some places that really lend themselves to
being soft, and sometimes, less often than we might like, we are
hard where they are not. I understand from some scientist friends
that there are also internal differences. Our jaw lines are different,
our pelvises differ, and somewhere I read that men have one less
rib. Linda insists that men have much harder heads.

There are many places where you can find out more about
these differences: *Playboy, Penthouse, Gallery*. But there are many
differences that I have not seen widely or carefully discussed,
perhaps because of tender ears or sensitivities. As you have come to
expect, I will boldly go where no man has previously gone. I should
also note that, as usual, our female counterparts have been thoroughly educated in all these differences in Woman School, while
we men muddle on hopelessly thinking *they* are the innocent ones.

For example, I once overheard a conversation between Daughter Antonia and Wife Linda; clearly a discussion of Woman School lessons from which I was intended to be excluded. Antonia commented that she was really getting edgy about traveling with Linda because Linda's radio is constantly turned to the whining and puling of a country music station. Antonia theorized, "I'm not sure, but I think your country music is interacting with my acne medicine."

I thought maybe she was just joking until I heard Linda reply with all seriousness and motherly love, "Could be. I know for a fact that rock and roll interacts with birth control pills."

I'm not even sure what that means, but I'm pretty sure it means something.

BEAUTY AND THE BEAST

Women are programmed to worry about beauty; men are programmed to notice it, elbow each other, ogle and google, whistle and hoot, drool and slobber but not to pay all that much attention to it when it comes right down to where they're going to sleep. If you believe what you hear from men, they like women who are skinny as skeletons but with gigantic mammary glands. Every man I know talks like that; every man I know pays no attention whatsoever to such things when settling on the woman he wants in his life.

Beauty, you know, is not an absolute. It varies widely from culture to culture. But curiously, what is consistent about beauty is that it tends to be whatever represents wealth. In the Middle Ages desireable women were rich and lived a life of ease in a stone castle, out of the sun, out of the fields, away from the smoke and dirt of ordinary life. So pale skin was the very essence of beauty, while in ballads of the time, "nutbrown maid" was understood to represent ugliness, even evil. These days the working girl sits in a cubicle in an office deep in the bowels of an office building while the rich girl plays golf and tennis, basks on the beaches of the Yucatan or the south of France. Brown girls are beautiful, while pale girls are working girls.

I'm not sure how that works with subcutaneous fat. In many cultures an obvious and rational demonstration of wealth, plenty, and ease is the well-marbled maiden—not only a symbol of her man's ability to feed her well, but also capable of surviving periods of need or childbirth. I'm not at all sure how the skinny girls in this world of supermodels, the Ally McBeals and the Lara FlynnBoyles, demonstrate wealth. Maybe it's just that they can afford to eat and then puke. I don't know.

What's important for us here is that we men really don't care all that much about a little extra padding here and there, but women do care. Never, ever, under any circumstances answer the question "Do you think I'm getting fat?" There is no acceptable answer. It's like the old conundrum, "Are you still beating your wife?" You are just going to get in trouble. Find something else to talk about. Immediately. Create a diversion. Spray a little charcoal lighter fluid on your pants and light yourself on fire, for example.

Sure, it's going to be painful, but not nearly as painful as saying something stupid like "Man, are you ever getting fat!" or "No, actually, not that fat," or "Actually, I *like* fat girls" or "Not as fat as Bart's wife Marcia, and I think she's hot," or "Roger Welsch says that in some cultures being fat represents wealth and is, therefore, beauty." It's just not going to work.

AMERICAN BEAUTY

What women don't understand at all is that any woman a man loves, or wants to love, is beautiful. Men figure that once they say "You are beautiful," it's like saying "I love you." The love has been established and doesn't need to be said over and over and over. Gents, take it from this expert. "I love you" *does* need to be said over and over and over. If you know what's good for you at all, you'd better just go ahead and say it over and over and over, no matter how silly you might feel. Say it, and mean it.

Chances are, if you truly love her, you'll be able to say it without a twinge of dishonesty. The bottom line is, women are beautiful, men are not. I'm not sure we need to know much more than that.

Shared Organs

Although men and women have some thoroughly delightful physical differences, we do share some of the same physical features—at least on the surface. For example, both species have ears, but we do not hear the same things. Women can hear male footsteps entering a house or apartment at 3:00 in the morning, when even the finest hunting dog hears nothing. They can hear a man ordering $120 worth of tools for his shop, even if he is calling from a pay phone two miles away.

Women hear you telling them that what they are wearing is perfectly lovely, they are not fat, and they are so radiantly beautiful, you love them more than ever, but their hearing memory is so weak, they can't recall that you told them that a day ago, or an hour ago. Women have told me that male hearing is designed to filter out soprano voices because they can remind the man in their lives to fix the drip in the bathroom faucet anywhere from fifty to a hundred times and he never seems to hear it once.

The Noses Have It

Female olfactory senses are also much heightened above the male. They can smell perfume they don't use on a man's coat after thirty days and two dry cleanings. Men can travel in a pickup truck together for two weeks, eating bean burritos and boiled eggs and drinking beer, stumble around in the woods looking for deer, poop behind trees, sleep with dogs, and not even come within a day's walk of a hot shower, and not one of them will detect the slightest whiff from his buddies. If he does accidentally wind up downwind from a particularly offensive emanation from either a buddy or one of the dogs, it will only arouse hilarity, glee, and good-natured admiration: "Hoo-ee, man! Did something just die in your pants? Did you get dragged ten miles behind a manure spreader? I've smelled sweeter than that from a Mexican sewage lagoon!"

A woman on the other hand will say things like, "Did you smoke a cigar?"

"Well, yes, a week ago Tuesday."

"Just as I thought. You are disgusting. You stink. Sleep on the porch."

THE EYES HAVE IT

Male and female eyes look a lot alike but couldn't be more different. A man doesn't notice that his shirt is misbuttoned, there is a smear of mustard on his nose, he shaved only one side of his face this morning, his wife changed from a blonde to a brunette since he left for work that morning, there's only a teaspoon of milk left in the bottom of the carton, and one of the kids has been missing for three days. On the other hand, he can spot a really great car or tractor buried in a clump of trees off the interstate a mile and a quarter at seventy miles an hour, a woman mooning the crowd from the upper stands at a packed Shea Stadium, a sale sign for Budweiser in bottles half-price at the back of the local liquor store even when the lights are turned out and it's snowing, and detect from 700 yards the very last copy of a *Sports Illustrated* swimsuit edition in a stack of 300 magazines, piled at random.

Women can see a hair a microshade different from theirs on a man's collar at the distance of a quarter mile, a woman wearing the same shoes at a full mile, a sale on cute figures of little children picking flowers at two miles, and a husband flirting with a barmaid in another state. Women cannot see an automobile's gas gauge or the little sticker that says when a car is due for service, a listing for a special Marathon Saturday of *COPS* in the local newspaper, a sign saying "Do not turn switch on while rotator drum is in motion," or reasons for attending a gun show.

EACH TO HIS OWN TASTE

Men like hot sauce and mustard, anchovies, raccoon sushi, Cajun jerky, Slim Jims, and, actually, almost anything you eat with your fingers and all things meat. Men love to cook if it involves fire and threatens explosions. Women like macaroni and cheese, tofu, sugar and spice and everything nice. Women would be amazed to learn what men eat in duck blinds, wilderness tents, and pickup trucks, and I strongly recommend that you men never-ever-never share this kind of information with any woman you intend to kiss.

Linda once came home early from grocery shopping and caught me eating goose jerky and Limburger cheese on rye bread, washed down with gin and tonic. For almost a week, she wouldn't even talk with me without wearing a respirator.

SEE ME, TOUCH ME, FEEL ME

Once again an ancient folkloric motif can remind us of universal truths. Remember the story about the princess and the pea? That's Linda and me. We react differently to small things. As in the fairy tale, she can get into bed and feel that there is a bread crumb that I must have dropped when I brought up the braunschweiger sandwiches and Pringles earlier in the day. On the other hand, I have gone upstairs, crawled into bed, and slept, only to find in the morning that I had left five or six rifles and handguns, some dismantled, lying about in the bed, with a couple clips and about a hundred rounds of loose ammo lying loose between the sheets.

This heightened sensitivity women suffer is apparently also the case with emotional conditions. Note the following sample conversations.

LINDA: Why were you flirting with that salesclerk?

ME: What salesclerk? I wasn't flirting with any salesclerk.

LINDA: You most certainly were flirting with her, the one back there in the appliances department.

ME: I just commented on how nice her bun warmers are.

LINDA: And you don't call that flirting?

ME: I call that shopping.

LINDA: You were sending out signals and I want you to stop.

ME: How can I stop sending out signals if I can't even tell that I *am* sending out signals?

LINDA: You are sending out signals and I want you to stop, right now.

ME: Okay, I've stopped.

LINDA: You're still sending out signals.

ME: How about now?

LINDA: Still . . . signals.

ME: Now?

LINDA: Even worse. Here. Step over here into the tool department. Fine. Now you're sending out tool signals. Okay. Don't let that happen again.

ME: Can I buy this breaker bar?

BLOOD BROTHERS

I am constantly asked about why men deal so poorly with illnesses but can be dropping blood by the bucket while deer hunting or working in the shop and not seem to notice. Here's the deal: cuts, slashes, abrasions, gouges, and divots are visible and localized. I mean, you know it's a cut, and it's bleeding. No problem. But a cold, flu, or other internal maladjustments are something entirely different.

Look at it this way: Antonia and I both get colds. When I get a cold, I have a 280-pound cold. Antonia only has a 120-pound cold. That's less than half the amount of cold by weight and volume than I have. Thus it is that I suffer far more with a cold than she does and require a lot more care and attention. I fail to see what is so complicated about that.

TIME AND TIME AGAIN

I've saved the issue of time, one of the most confusing problems between the male and female physiologies for last, in large part because I don't have a lot of answers. You can be sure that our researchers here at the Man School Research Institute for Gender Disparities are devoting a lot of time and energy to this problem and perhaps we will have an answer soon, but right now the issue is very confused. I do know that a woman can say she will be ready to go in "five minutes," and a half hour later I'm still standing there in a coat and galoshes waiting for her to come out of the bathroom. Okay, that's fine, but then why is she so bewildered and huffy when I say I'd come to the supper table after the last five minutes of this football game and show up a half hour later?

Why does a woman understand the amount of time embodied in the phrase "an hour's shopping" but not understand apparently at all the parallel construct "an hour up at the tavern"? Beats me.

A BUTT-COVERING AFTERWORD

A ll that being said, let it be noted that no one loves women more than I do. Metaphorically speaking. Linda has made it quite clear that metaphorical is just about the only kind of lady loving I'm going to be doing from now on. We had been married less than a year, I was still teaching at the University of Nebraska, and a lilting-voiced young lady from one of the campus sororities called one evening in early December and asked if I would be willing to come to their house and be Santa for their annual Christmas party.

My role, she explained, would be to sit in a big chair while her sorority sisters came forward to sit on my lap and tell me if they had been good girls, or bad girls, or really deliciously wonderfully adventuresome bad girls that year. Then I would make some kind of remarks about what sort of penances they would have to pay for their indiscretions or what rewards they deserved for being good girls.

University teachers are constantly being urged to spend more time with students, to get to know them, to show them professors are regular folks, to demonstrate that, scholars or not, we have interests well beyond our classroom and research duties. Well, this struck me as being precisely that kind of opportunity.

I figured it would be simply a matter of form to pass the idea by Linda, so I put my hand over the telephone and yelled, "Hey, Love! It's the Phelta Thi sorority and they would like me to be Santa for their Christmas party this year." I assumed that she would simply yell back, "Fine, dear. That would be nice. Have a good time. Don't wake me up when you come in."

Well, that was not her reaction at all. My recollection, insofar as I can remember anything about the event through the haze of post-traumatic stress syndrome, was that she grabbed the phone, and with a thin, steely voice sent the sweet sorority girl back to her pledge class sobbing, cut off my flesh in square-inch patches with laser sabers glaring from the pupils of her eyes, and through telepathic messages seared onto the cortex of my brain clear instructions never to so much as think of such depravities again, ever. So much for the spirit of Christmas.

This book is not an attack on women. I love women. In fact, if you read it carefully, this is a book about men. I don't understand women at all. What can I say about women? So don't write me ugly letters about me being a clod, pig, lout, cad, cur, slob, or a jerk. I know all those things. I've been told them before by women I love—mothers, wives, daughters. I've written books about how frustrating it is to work with old tractors and how much I love old tractors. That's what I'm saying here too. I adore women. I think they are wonderful. And wonderfully mysterious. And wonderfully frustrating. I am a lot of things, but I am definitely not a woman-hater. In fact, I look around me and wonder how I could possibly have been kept around by the women in my life.

You know, a beehive is a remarkable model for social behavior: there is a queen, who rules everything in her realm, and she is surrounded by thousands of workers, gathering honey and pollen, feeding the young, tending the queen, cleaning the hive, doing everything that needs to be done to keep the community humming along—and they are all women.

Occasionally, in the spring, these women work their magic and make sure some males are born to the hive. (Only the queen can make babies, by the way.) The males are called drones. They don't do a thing but sit around, eat, and poop.

Except for one. One drone has a special job assignment in that hive. If the old queen should die or wear out, a new queen is selected for the hive. If she is going to be the Queen Mother Bee, she needs to make babies. And to make babies, she needs a male. So she selects a handsome young male, taps him on the shoulder, tells him he is so smart and cute and clever and funny and wonderful and strong, and wouldn't he like to fly high into the sky with her and have his macho way with her.

Of course, being a male, the drone says "You betcha!" They fly off, high into the sky. She embraces him, he has a wonderful orgasm, and then she kills him. She returns to the hive to conduct her business of running things and having babies the rest of her life.

A couple drones are kept around the hive just in case the ladies need to inseminate another queen, but when autumn rolls around and the workers have to start thinking about who is going to be eating and working, and who is just sitting around eating and pooping, they turn their eyes to the drones, who are buzzing, "Who? Me?"

The ladies kill all the men and throw their corpses out the front door onto the ground. The next spring, if the lady workers decide they need males, they'll just make some. No big deal.

Frankly, I think this is the direction we are heading as a species. A recent Reuters news item from Adelaide, Australia, reported that researchers there had figured out a way to fertilize an egg with cells from *any* part of the body, *any* body, rather than *specific* parts of a *specific* body. The article further speculates that this would make it possible for a woman to be the father of her own child, which would save a lot of problems, especially when it comes to court decisions on child support and the ever-abhorred wet spot. Presumably, a woman could now have her next child fathered by a butt pimple, which some women I know would applaud as preferable to the current arrangement vis-à-vis the butt pimples in their lives.

A woman I know and have expressed some affection for now and again has said quite truthfully that okay, men never seem to notice when a woman has changed her hair color, adopted a new dress style, or lost a limb; similarly, women wouldn't notice if men dropped off the face of the earth.

What's scary about this is that I understand it totally. I look around me and see maybe ten men who understand what incredible good fortune they have that some woman they most certainly do not deserve has for some reason decided to keep them on through the winter and breed with them more than once.

I'm not going to excuse man behavior, except to say to you ladies who happen to read this, that we don't know any better. That is not much of an excuse, but it's the only excuse we have. What is remarkable to me is that there are women who tolerate this and even deal with it successfully.

CONSIDER THIS WELL

Right off the top of my head, I can think of a couple dozen male slobs who treat their beautiful, intelligent wives like hired girls. Or worse, like field mules. Nah, I take that back. No man would treat a valuable asset like a mule that poorly.

I look at these guys and really wonder what goes on in their heads. Do they not see in their women what I see? If not, then I reckon they aren't going to have those women very long, because some other guy as smart as me but younger and less committed is going to run off with them, sure as hell. Believe it or not, I *hope* that is the case, because the alternative is that these men think they are so wonderful, handsome, sexy, desirable, and cute that the women in their lives don't deserve them! This would be such an incredibly stupid arrogance, I have a hard time even grasping it.

Here's the deal about this book and therefore about Man School: you can read this and laugh, but you better also do some thinking about it. Chuckle all you want, make jokes about the Little Lady, call her Precious Moments and laugh behind your hand, leave that toilet lid up, fart and belch at will, but that better be nothing much more than public display and a total act. In private, you better be making it clear to the woman that you understand your unworthiness, that you are daily grateful for her forbearance, that you may joke but you know full well on which side your bread is buttered, and that you may nibble and lick the hand that feeds you but would never for a moment consider biting it.

Learn the lesson of the bees, my lads. Have a little bee tattooed on the back of your right hand so that every time you do anything at all, you are reminded exactly where you stand and how utterly unworthy you are.

I'm not talking here about crawling and cringing. Be as macho as you want. Just remember the truth, and whenever you can, make the little gestures. My friend, Bob, is the dumbest guy I know along these lines. He has it exactly wrong. There's absolutely no way in hell this clod deserves the gorgeous woman he has. She is beautiful, bright, and makes a damn good living. He is balding, clunky, and utterly clueless about anything remotely refined.

Now, it's not like she asks him to grow hair, lose 100 pounds, get an M.A. in art history, and buy a suit. No, she asks for things like something less than warp speed on the interstate in the wreckage he calls his pickup truck, a call home when he is on the road for more than a week, some appreciation for how exhausted she is when she comes home from her ferociously demanding job, an occasional gesture of recognition of her existence on weekends when there are thirty-seven football games on television.

I love this guy, and I understand his sense of priorities, but I also know what his chances are of bagging another prize like his wife, Frieda. Zip. Zero. Nada. None. He simply cannot afford to let this one go. He not only is not going to do any better, he's never again going to do this well.

Make that his "first wife Frieda." After enduring this dolt for three years she finally had enough and moved on. Okay, yeah, she moved on to yet another, even worse jerk, but that seems to be the way of the world of a woman willing to accept a man in her life. As

I have taught my daughter from her earliest years of understanding, "All men are pigs."

But the main thing is, if the clod of the first part had demonstrated even the slightest recognition of how lucky he was, if he had made even the most pathetic, even symbolic gestures at acknowledging this woman's value, he'd still be sitting in the catbird seat with her. As it is, with even less to offer than he had five years ago, he is once again out there on the market, trying after years of being out of practice to fake sensitivity and charm.

This friend of mine needs to take a minute every day and consider how incredibly lucky he was and act accordingly. He needs to walk by a beehive in late autumn and kick his way through the drifts of dead drones. That's what I do. Linda doesn't ask much, but a lot of what she asks is really silly: the toilet lid thing, the fish guts on the ceiling thing, the picking up my underwear thing, the sorting the laundry thing, the all-the-light-switches-either-up-or-down thing. That's okay. When I consider where I would be without her, even for a week, those little quirks and peculiarities really look like trivial expectations from this old boy. So I do them.

As you leave these hallowed halls of Man School, graduates, that's your first assignment. Pay attention. Consider the kind of prize you are as a man in any woman's life. Imagine being without her. Act accordingly.

A TWELVE-STEP PROGRAM FOR RELATIONSHIPS

I'm not a fan of twelve-step programs, or any kind of programs for that matter except for programs about robot wars, spring break in Acapulco, and *COPS*. Self-help has never appealed to me because I'm not sure there is much help for me, and, I'd be the last guy I'd turn to for help, even for myself. I wouldn't recommend that anyone else listen to much I have to say about love, sex, romance, and marriage, so why would I listen to it myself? I realize that it's pretty late in this book to tell you that my opinions aren't worth much, but you probably figured out pretty early that: 1) I don't know what I'm talking about; 2) you don't either, but you still probably know more than I do; and 3) if you are a typical American male, you are so damn desperate at this point you're willing to listen to almost anyone, including me.

What's more, not only do I not know anything about women and precious little about human beings, I know even less about twelve-step programs. I once developed a twelve-step program for some friends of mine who are obsessive-compulsive, for example. Actually, it only has one step, but you repeat it twelve times. My only exposure to twelve-step programs has been from other people who are working their way through one, and when they get to the step where they need to apologize to someone, they almost automatically think of me.

Something about me attracts apologies. (It has also become uncomfortably evident to me over the past twenty years how many friends of mine suffer from clinical depression. I'm sure it's just a coincidence.) My favorite was from the woman who sought to redeem her pathetic self with an apology that mostly said, "I'm really sorry that I made such a point about what a cosmic, insufferable, irredeemable, eternal asshole you are." It must be nice to cleanse your psyche like that. I know I sure felt better after I read her letter.

I'm not an expert in psychology and, unlike Dr. Laura Schlessinger, I'm not dishonest enough to pretend that I am. I'm not even sure there is such a thing as psychology. At any rate, I hope to develop eventually a curriculum for Man School with a twelve-step program for manhood, but for the purposes of this encyclopedic volume dealing with relationships, I am going to start with a twelve-step approach for men dealing specifically with relationship problems. Follow these steps faithfully, meet in little groups, bare your soul, have a couple beers and Slim Jims and get back to me. I'm uneasy about trying this kind of thing until I have some idea where it's going:

I. The notion of self-management is nonsense. We are powerless not only in regard to alcohol, tobacco, sex, and salted peanuts, we are powerless in the altogether. The sooner we recognize that, the sooner we can move on to dealing with powerlessness. In fact, if we intend to succeed in a relationship, the first thing we have to do is accept helplessness in our love and trust for the other person in the relationship—our woman. If she will do the same. If she won't, do what she does and pretend.

Most twelve-step programs tell you you are in charge.

Well, you'd have to be a drunk or a nut to believe that. You're getting nowhere in a relationship until you realize and admit that without this woman, you're nothing. Without her, you're not even you.

2. There may be a power greater than us who can restore us to sanity. Or in contrast to what other twelve-step programs try to tell you, there may not be. Actually, when it comes right down to it, sanity may not be all it's cracked up to be. And what's sanity have to do with male-female relationships anyway, what with testosterone and estrogen?

3. You have to be nuts to believe in sanity. As other programs suggest, we probably should admit our wrongs, but then if we knew what our wrongs were, wouldn't we most likely not have done them in the first place? So, how do we know what's wrong now if we didn't know what was wrong before? Probably the best thing to do is be nice. That would do it.

Forget the past, because either the other guy has, or would like to, or can't. And don't do an apology in which you simply make yourself feel better by reiterating your previous obnoxious behavior. A relationship is more a matter of naked souls than naked bodies. If the honesty isn't there, neither is the relationship. Apologies are no more than a fart in a tornado. Don't bother to apologize. Just don't do it again.

6. Admit that no one can remove any faults in our character but us. If you're counting on God to do it, it ain't gonna happen. It's like blaming farts on dogs. You can do it, but no one is going to believe you. Least of all, the dogs. Among all the other things we have been blessedly given is a brain. Using it is the closest you can come to a perfect prayer.

7. You can ask God to remove your shortcomings—or ask the garbage service, or Congress, or a plastic surgeon. Won't make any difference. The first thing to do is give some serious thought to whether they really are shortcomings. If you listen to others, the fact that you drive below the speed limit during an ice storm on the interstate during rush hour is a shortcoming. Other people are idiots. Your shortcoming may be listening to others to decide what your shortcomings are.

    On the other hand, even if they think you have shortcomings, you have to decide how important they are. A blue-haired widow in Omaha thinks I should cut my hair. Who cares? I think she should lose some weight and subscribe to *Penthouse.* The woman I love thinks I should rinse out my glass whenever I drink buttermilk. Easy enough. You got it, babe. That glass is going to be rinsed, every time.

8. Don't ask amends from anyone who doesn't deserve to be asked. If you have insulted or injured someone who deserves it, more power to you. Why not make a list of other people who need to be told what assholes they are? And then tell them? What's more important is to consider those whom you love but haven't told often enough.

    Forget the jerks you have flipped off in the past. Let's consider the ones we love but haven't hugged lately. Americans are more than ready to give the finger to somebody they've never seen before and may never see again. How about we make a point of doing the opposite and telling someone we love that we love them. Or even just wave a friendly wave to someone on the streets and highways. I think that's a lot more important than making up to some idiot we once thought deserved a snarl. We can start with the good folks maybe and work our way down to the jerks.

9. Be an asset to the good and, what is equally important, a horror to the evil. What good does it do to be cozy with the nicies if we are going to tolerate the scumbags? If you are spending time pounding emotionally, metaphorically, or physically, on the woman in your life, what kind of idiot are you? Too lazy to move on? Too dumb to sort it out? If you're not happy, save everyone a lot of trouble and find someone else. There is someone else. Well, maybe not for all of you . . .

10. Be ready to accept and correct your own failings, but don't ignore the same things in others. Get rid of that kind of baggage, or make a point of noting it to the offender. Down the road they'll be grateful that you pointed out their obvious character faults. Well, okay, no they won't, actually. They will always hate you for your honesty. As a matter of fact, they will never change. It won't take much more than a high school reunion to make this clear to you. But damn, will it ever make you feel better! Conversely, if you never say what is obvious to you, and probably others, you will regret it the rest of your life.

   All kidding aside, the most important thing about all this twelve-step crapola is that we admit our limited knowledge. I have always insisted that we can determine the degree to which a religion is wrong by the degree to which it insists it is right. And that is the absolute truth. Same in marriage or love. The more a person insists on inerrancy, the more likely fallibility is. Just admit that you're an idiot. Because you are an idiot. Sure, so is your woman. And once she admits the same thing, you can kiss and make up. Maybe even more—a nuzzle here, nibble there. Then your faults really become evident. And the solution too which is, none of that matters.

11. You can pray all you want (Let me head off the zealots' screams at this point I believe in prayer more than you do—much

more—and I consider myself to be profoundly religious, more than you, street-corner Pharisee!), but you can't rely on God(s) to sort out your problems. God not only gave you a dick, he gave you a brain. You are, therefore, not only destined to breed, you are given the mechanisms to control your breeding. You can spend all the time you want on your knees asking for God to straighten out your relationship but there's a pretty good chance he's going to shrug his shoulders and say something like "You're the dumbshit who got yourself into this fix, so get yourself out. I have better things to do: moving the galaxies, keeping the sun's fires stoked, sorting out Tarot cards."

12. Not all twelve-step programs have twelve steps. Or, for that matter, eleven.

Forget about instructing the others. You have more than enough to do sorting out your own miserable self and your relationship. The arrogant notion that you can do anything for anyone else is idiotic. Go put up a table in the local tavern and start advising people on how they can be better. When you recover from your wounds, when you get out of jail, when your eyes open again, when you can walk, go back and do it again. Do that until you've figured out that you should mind your own business. Then take a look at yourself. Lots to be done there, huh? And how about your relationships? Not exactly perfect? Why don't we start there and only when you have your own life figured out start to straighten out everyone else?

Not long ago there was an article in our local paper about a plump little small-town dumpling who was headed off on a missionary bus to southern Mexico to bring righteousness and truth to benighted Mayan natives. I have spent some time among the Mayan, and in southern Mexico. I winced. She said she hoped to bring the message of blessings of hard work and worship to the Mayans there. I kept thinking that someone who loved this innocent, ignorant boob should shoot her and save her the embarrassment that was sure to come. She wouldn't last an hour in the kind of labor the Mayans do. And less than that under the blinding glare of their devotion and worship.

Only her innocence and arrogance let her believe she was in any way even close to a par with them on either basis. I'm betting that pasty-skinned, flabby-fleshed, superficially spiritual child came back either shattered by her experience or convinced that she had been tortured by Satan worshipers in an effort to divert her from the True Faith.

Same with relationships, folks. You can ask God all you want to sort out your problems, but it just could be that God gave you the mechanisms and figures you should have the sense to use them to handle things yourself. The very last thing, the very most unlikely thing, for you to even consider is to foist your pathetic ignorances off on others before you deal with them yourself.

How do I know? Because I'm just as dumb as you are, that's how. And you and I are smarter than most.

A FRIENDLY
GUIDE FOR
WOMEN
TRYING TO
GET A MAN TO
GO TO A
MOVIE

I recommend that you photocopy the material below and distribute it to the women in your life, not simply to help them in their efforts to wheedle their way into your life and love but also to help you out, since it just may get you out of an hour's worth of *Oprah* or worse yet, a whole damn movie of something with Molly Ringwald about relationships and love (without nudity) and conversations and inner meanings and self-exploration.

Ladies, listen up a second, okay? Through deception and temptation you may be able to get that man in your life to go to some wretched movie about relationships and romantic love with you today, but in the long run it is just going to make things a lot harder the next time. If you apply the following test to the movie you are about to inflict on this wretched lout of yours, you will have some idea of what your chances are going to be of ever getting him past a movie lobby again for the rest of your relationship, which is probably already a lot more tenuous than you are thinking.

Consider the following alternatives for the movie you are thinking of dragging him to. Keep track of the cumulative score.

Does the movie contain female nudity?
Lots = +30
Some = +20
None, but some tight skirts and wet blouses = +10
Yeah, but it's Calista Flockhart = −10

Does the movie contain male nudity?
Lots, and mostly guys with implants = −30 points
Some, but mostly butts = −20
Some, but only in conjunction with female nudity = wash
Yes, but it's Woody Allen = +10

Chases?
Trucks, motorcycles, cars, and airplanes = +30
Foot chases mostly but with a woman not wearing a bra = +20
Dog chases a guy and bites him real good = +10
Yes, but on ice skates = −20

Explosions?
Most of the film consists of explosions, some in midair = +30
Only two, but one includes a woman not wearing a bra = +20
No explosions but a couple of good car crashes = +10
Only in the kitchen = −20

Weapons used in filming . . .
Artillery, machine guns, lasers, neutron dilithium disintegrators,

etc. = +30

Pistols, rifles, maybe a hand grenade or two = +20

Knives, clubs, rocks, spears = +10

Paint guns, snowballs = —10

Theater?

Jammed, scantily clad sorority girls on summer break = +30

No one but you and the hottie you're dating = +20

You, your girlfriend, and six of your buddies = +10

Crowded with children on a school field trip = —30

Served in the lobby . . .

5-gal buckets of butter-soaked popcorn, liter mugs of beer = +50

Permission to bring your own coolers = +40

Good and Plenties, pork rinds, huge Cokes, free refills = +30

HoHos and Kool-Aid, but served by topless babes = +20

Yogurt cups, tofu on a stick = —20

ADD UP YOUR SCORE.

Anything over 180: Dump the turkey you're with, and send your name and phone number to this author marked FOR IMMEDIATE ATTENTION.

140–180: You can count on seeing another movie with this guy and if you are at all interested in marrying him, immediately following this date would be a good time to make the suggestion.

120–140: Unless you scored real high in the last two items of this inventory, it's going to be a long, long time before you get him to another movie, so make sure your account is solid at Video Kingdom.

100–120: Depending on where exactly you piled up the negative points in the above inventory, you may want to consider organizing a local chapter of the Oprah Winfrey Chic Flick Society. There's no way in hell you are going to get this guy to go to another movie with you, ever.

Below 100: Saturday nights are a good time to reorganize closets and trim cuticles, they tell me.

CATALOG OF MATERIALS FOR ADDITIONAL MAN SCHOOL STUDY

Many of you will ask, "Okay, Doctor Love, when I have finished working my way through your book, have taken all the evaluation tests, filled out the forms, studied the examples and diagrams, then what more can I do to make myself as successful in love, sex, romance, and marriage as you are?"

For one thing, start saving your money for the next volume of this encyclopedia. Secondly, make a copy of the list below and start assembling your own library of materials to help you be a real man and to find and please a real woman. Here are some additional materials you can consider in your educational endeavors.

Let's start with audio visuals. You should have on hand, not rented but purchased, several examples of films with W.C. Fields or Mae West. You just should. Everyone should. You should also have at least one film on hand that captures what you want the world to be like and use it as regular therapy. For me that is a very obscure Paul Newman film, *Quintet*. It makes the world look pretty terrible, but in the end the hero, Newman, leaves the ugliness of "civilized" life and wanders back out onto the Ice Age ice cap. And that's what I want to do.

Well, to my own astonishment, one of my favorite films in this world has no car chases, explosions, or sex, and the only nudity is a brief glimpse of Catherine Zeta-Jones' obviously delicious backside—*High Fidelity*. I cannot praise this film too much. The language is really rough, but it's all about relationships and romance and even has a fuzzy, warm conclusion.

Don't get me wrong: this is no chick flick. I watched it with both Antonia and Linda, and at the end, when I was checking to see if I hadn't laughed my hiatal hernia back into action, they sat there with nothing but bewilderment on their faces. In short, this is a nonaction movie men absolutely love and which women don't get at all. It is definitely not a film to which I would take a date, maybe not even a girlfriend or spouse. It's a man film. And I think maybe it is best seen when you are alone so no one will see you cry. And believe me, you will cry when you see Catherine Zeta-Jones' delicious backside.

PRINTED MATTER

Cabela's Catalog or any similar outdoor gear resource. This item is more than mere entertainment. If you persist in trying to hook up with a woman, you are almost certainly going to wind up spending some time sleeping under a tree or back porch.

Tool catalog. Same here, but there is also considerable entertainment value in a publication that: 1) you enjoy, and 2) she does not emjoy.

Skin magazines—*Playboy*, *Penthouse*, and some old *National Geographics*—strictly for the articles, of course.

Tractor operators manual, shop manuals. These are not only wonderful reading, they get better as you get older. And you can also use them to conceal the skin magazines.

Bible (or, at least, the Song of Solomon). You'll be surprised how much good reading there is in these pages, and so would the Baptists who have all their lives only read or heard very atypical selected passages!

Kama Sutra. Contrary to what you may think, this will not be nearly as useful in coming up with new and exciting sexual tricks as it will be in making you laugh like crazy.

Don't bother with a dictionary. When you're dealing with women, it really doesn't matter what words mean. If you insist on knowing what words mean, get a copy of Ambrose Bierce's *The Devil's Dictionary*. This is all you'll ever need to know about words.

Anything from Oprah's book club. If you read any of these selections, you will understand 1) how women think, 2) why women think the way they do, and 3) why you should thank your lucky stars you are not a woman.

Almanac. No particular reason other than this is some of the best reading around.

Menus for food delivery. Some things from your single past may have to be surrendered but not good eating. Besides, sooner or later she is going to have to go out of town and leave you alone, and then it's time for some great anchovy and pepperoni pizza, Szechuan beef, that kind of thing.

Keep your old address book. Same thing: sooner or later . . .

The Sirens of Titan. The book that most clearly and hilariously captures the meaning of life (other than the Bible's Song of Solomon) is Kurt Vonnegut's *The Sirens of Titan*. I can't even think about this book without laughing hilariously, shaking my head until my eyes rattle, and hoping to everything that is beautiful and true that our purpose in this universe is precisely as delineated by Vonnegut.

Jim Harrison's writing is pretty tough stuff, but I do recommend his book on food and eating, *The Raw and the Cooked*. It's not as good as my own *Diggin' in & Piggin' Out*, but Jim is my friend and I think you should buy his books because sooner or later he'll get back out here again and spend some of his royalty monies taking me out to eat, drink, and look at naked girls dancing on a stage.

Finally, I hope you will keep up on my books and other things by checking my Web site, currently at agriculture.com/welsch/roger/. A list of all my books can be found there, along with a biography.

The following is an excerpt from Roger Welsch's latest book Outhouses *(ISBN 0-7603-1149-8). It is available from MBI Publishing. To purchase a copy, call 1.800.826.6600, or else visit our website at motorbooks.com.*

Introduction

"For this relief, much thanks. . . ."
—William Shakespeare
Hamlet, act I, scene I

I've never understood why so many scenes in movies, novels, and plays focus on events in the bedroom when the fact of the matter is, the bathroom is the most interesting room in the house. No room in the house is furnished with quite so many unique and curious items as the bathroom. A bedroom in Paris is, well, a bedroom. It has, for example, a bed. But a bathroom in Paris can be almost anything but is very likely to be a substantial departure from what you have grown up with considering your standard bathroom equipment in Sheboygan, Wisconsin!

To be sure, there are regional differences in the *salle de bain* in America, or at different economic levels. On a couple occasions I have been a guest in some pretty tony hotels in major American cities, for example. The sleeping area is fairly standard: a bed with sheets and a cover, maybe twin beds; a bedside table with a telephone, a clock, and a lamp; maybe a desk, maybe a table. Sometimes there is a couch, sometimes a recliner, perhaps only a chair. There is a longish, largish dresser of sorts with drawers, maybe a television set perched atop it. That's pretty much it. Not a lot of surprises there.

But now let's take a look into the "private room." Why is it that some hotels consider a shower cap a basic freebie, while others do not? Why does one Holiday Inn provide me with body lotion, and another thinks I should have a shoe polishing cloth instead? Shouldn't we pretty much have the fundamental showerhead standardized by now? So why are there big ones that gush and little ones that squirt, and throbbers and stingers and drippers? Why are there sometimes two faucets to adjust and on others only one? Why do we sometimes push for water, other times pull, or turn, or twist? And couldn't we all agree on how to turn the water from the tub spigot to the showerhead?

And what is this here? A magnifying glass with a built-in light? And a hair dryer? Okay, that's nice, but what is this I see here? A telephone? Who got the idea of putting a telephone by the toilet? I don't want to talk to anyone while I'm, well, you know, and I don't want them talking to me at that delicate time either, and to be perfectly honest, I am almost absolutely certain no one wants to talk with *me* while I am indisposed, as the phrase goes, so what I am really curious about is, who does use the phone whilst seated on the throne?

On second thought, maybe I don't want to know.

And what's the deal with the little envelope fold at the end of the toilet paper? Is that for something? If so, I don't know what it is, and I just don't feel comfortable asking the young woman at the front desk. After you use paper, are you expected to put that little fold back in the paper for the next person? Toilet seat up, toilet seat down? Throw used towels on the floor, fold them neatly in the corner of the vanity top, hang them back on the rack? Do you get to take all the little freebies—sewing kit, shower cap, body lotion—with you even if you don't use them? Will the lady who cleans the room notice that the hotel shampoo is gone, but there is no empty shampoo container in the bathroom wastebasket? Will she think less of you if you take it with you, rather than using it in her shower?

We don't even know what to call these places that are so neces-sary that they have in our recent past been called a "necessary." Ladies' room, men's room. How's *that* for a locution? Why ladies but not gentlemen? *Rest* room? Is *rest* a really good term for what we do there when often it actually requires no small effort? Powder room? Little boys' room? Relief station? Pit stop?

What's more, some of us have our doubts about the multi-tasking we, at least we Americans, have brought to this, the small-est room of our home, pooping, bathing, brushing our teeth, storing our medicines, performing morning and evening ablu-tions, applying makeup, in some motels and hotels making coffee, for Pete's sake, and—please, dear Lord, let it be—reading. No wonder there is a tacit theory that personalities are formed and shattered here. No one says, "He is a very rich man because he once had a couple weeks of problems in the bedroom, if you catch my drift, in his younger years, so he's never gotten over it and he therefore drives his employees like sled dogs to make up for this momentary lapse of vigor." No, but people do say, "Yeah, sure, he's rich, anal retentive you know." No further explanation needed. We all know what that means, and we all know where it happened. Or, as the case is, didn't happen. "He must have been a real problem in potty training."

I know what is happening at this very moment—your mind is flying from one of your acquaintances to another, probably to your employer, as you acknowledge that bathroom behavior or nonbehav-ior is a solid determinant for later personality development. Our bathrooms then are a good deal more than small spaces set aside for putting aside. Yes, our toilets are places where heroes and villains of our societies are made and broken; they therefore deserve far more credit and attention than we have given them, anthropologically, philosophically, spiritually, intellectually, poetically.

And that's what I'm about to do in these pages. This is not simply a book about outhouses, however, or even about elimination. This is a book for reading in your outhouse, but is also an apology and appeal for the return, refurbishing (in both architecture and reputation) of not simply the outhouse in its more restricted manifestations but of the privy in its more general manifestations too, whether that be a New York hotel bathroom—a windowless, sterile, uninspiring, echoing, cold place of little comfort, or that wonderfully airy, open, natural, inviting, friendly, sheltering comfort of the rural chapel. Brought to my own farm outhouse by the gentle urgings of my metabolism, about which I promise you will read little more in these pages, I have devoted some considerable time to thinking about the meaning of life and man and outhouses and a thousand other issues, which I now present to you.

Why the outhouse? Why not my shop, which has after all inspired a half dozen other books? Why not the living room of our home where I spend many hours within the bosom of my family? Why not the kitchen, which is the real heart of any genuine American home? Or the patio? Or, certainly more logically, our automobile? Well, because I do my most and best philosophical thinking in the bathroom, inspired by a daily bathroom reconnection with my fundamental nature—my basic humanity, and the time to consider it. And this is a book of essays thus inspired.

No matter how frantic our days, no matter what problems beset our families, no matter how oppressive our associations with other human beings or nature, no matter what, there comes a time when we are required by our very most basic natures to stop, sit, and, like it or not, relax. And inevitably, to think. The essays in this little book result from my own musings during my daily moments of introspection, and my sincerest hope is that you will read and consider them during yours. In a way, this book is an experiment in communication. Perhaps in these moments of mutual identity, we, you and I, will understand each other better than at any other time of our day, any other moment of our otherwise very different lives.

Despite all the clichés, laughter is not a universal language; around the world we laugh at very different things, and sometimes, cruelly, at each other. Food is certainly not universal. We gag and retch when confronted with what other people eat, and they condemn us to hell for eating the most vile of foods, forbidden by various and sundry gods. Music is not only not a universal language, the howling and whining my beloved wife Linda calls music is enough to bring me to emptying a shotgun into a radio— even a car radio. Beauty is not international, not even spanning the gap from one generation to another.

Is there anything we humans do that we universally share, that we all do, that we all do pretty much the same, that we all find comfort and relief in, men and women, young and old, regardless of religion, nationality, or race? Of course there is. We all poop and pee. And we all poop and pee fundamentally in pretty much the same way—fundamentally. Perhaps in this small niche, mankind can at last be brought together in a renewed kinship. Language, religion, sex, customs, those things all separate us, but maybe in the communality of the irresistible geologic pressures of yesterday's supper—be that bean curry or Cajun gumbo or Minnesota lutefisk or a peanut-butter-and-jelly sandwich—we are all brought to the same place and put in the same position— seated—in a bathroom. Pretty inspirational, huh? Talk about a "fellowship of man!" No matter how different we are at any other point along our alimentary canal, when it comes right down to it, as it were, we are fundamentally, so to speak, the same.

While that union of man is true in terms of the process, the preference of venue for that process is not so universal. I have conducted a scientific survey of upward of two dozen modern, living human beings who have used an outhouse, and the results are dramatic and conclusive: most men figure an outhouse is just fine (although men are generally pretty much content to do their alimentary leavings wherever the spirit moves them, including in public places) while women universally would rather just hold it for a week or 10 days, rather than use an outhouse. Now that I think about it, that may be one of the very reasons men find an outhouse so inviting—in an outhouse there are few women, which also means there will be no rappings at the door in midrelaxation, no wet panty-hose hanging in the immediate area of the front-row seating, no diaper buckets sending forth their distinctive reekings, no discomforting thoughts about what is happening below you while your toothbrush hangs only a yard away, no medicine cabinets clogged with vials insisting that the contents be used up before the end of World War I, no makeup kits, no hair tints, shampoos, conditioners, body emulsifiers, split-end menders, root stimulators, follicle refurbishers, dandruff tonics, highlight refreshers, luster enhancers, blah, blah, blah. . . .

Thus, the male species—and men and women are indeed separate species no matter what misguided biologists may think in this matter—is not only driven from the in-house relief station by the overwhelming occupation and influence of his female counterpart(s), he is welcomed to his outhouse by their parallel absence there. Man, is that a tidy paradigm, or what?

Nope, an outhouse is, as the book by Chic Sales so long ago made clear, a place of specialization. One poops and pees in an outhouse. And does some reading and thinking, of course too, but that's about it. It's a place where a man can enjoy his solitary thoughts, a perfect literary irony, the most spacious and free room of the homestead, and yet by far and away the smallest. There surely is a poetic message there somewhere.

Besides, the outhouse has traditionally been the place for the forbidden mysteries. Archaeologists love locating ancient outhouses, because long-gone clients of the little buildings saw them not simply as relief stations for evacuating the bowels but also for lubricating them. An ancient privy pit is a great place to find ancient liquor bottles, stashed out there by the Old Man, emptied, and then discarded deep into that dark recess where the Little Lady would never look, no matter how bright the sunshine. (To be perfectly honest, however, the frequency of finds involving high-alcohol elixirs for "female complaints" suggest that many of our grandmothers also found the outhouse a convenient place for indulging one's appetites.) More by accident, old privy pits are also the archaeologist's favorite place to look for lost firearms; the process seems obvious: a pistol carried loosely in the pocket falls easily out and with the unerring certainty of a dropped toothbrush goes inevitably down the hole and deep into the morass below.

Same with the lingerie section from the Sears catalog or the *Police Gazette,* which could be stashed out there in the outhouse and examined with delicious care. Even today my own outhouse has a tin box, originally a kitchen bread box, I think, in which I keep some extra reading materials, if you catch my drift, a couple Swisher Sweet cigars, and a small flask of Jack Daniel's Black Label Tonic for Gentleman's Complaint. But don't tell Linda. She doesn't know about such things.

INDEX